A METAPHORICS
OF FICTION

A METAPHORICS OF FICTION

DISCONTINUITY AND DISCOURSE IN THE MODERN NOVEL

ALAN SINGER

A FLORIDA STATE UNIVERSITY
BOOK/TALLAHASSEE
University Presses of Florida

Library of Congress Cataloging in Publication Data

Singer, Alan, 1948–
    A metaphorics of fiction.

    "A Florida State University book."
    Bibliography: p.
    Includes index.
    1. Fiction—Technique.   2. Metaphor.   I. Title.
PN3383.M48M4   1984   808.3   83-16860
ISBN 0–8130–0773–9 (alk. paper)

University Presses of Florida, the agency of the State of Florida's university system for the publication of scholarly and creative works, operates under the policies adopted by the Board of Regents. Its offices are located at 15 Northwest 15th Street, Gainesville, Florida 32603.

Typography by G & S Typesetters, Austin, Texas

Printed in U.S.A. on acid-free paper

CONTENTS

Preface	ix
1. The Fictions of Metaphor	1
2. The Metaphors of Fiction	23
3. The Horse Who Knew Too Much: Metaphor and the Narrative of Discontinuity in *Nightwood*	47
4. The Parody of Fate: *Second Skin* and the Death of the Novel	79
5. The Need of the Present: *How It Is* with the Subject in Beckett's Novel	115
6. Narrative as Event and Act	157
Notes	171
Selected Bibliography	177
Index	181

But the greatest thing by far is to be a master of metaphor. It is the one thing that cannot be learnt from others . . . .

Aristotle

PREFACE

This work concerns itself with the productive, disseminative power of linguistic rhetoricity, its relation to the concept of fiction and to the practice of the novel in the twentieth century. What follows should therefore be methodologically distinguished from the related projects of a rhetoric of fiction on the one hand and formalist genre study on the other. I present neither a systematic esthetic philosophy of the novel nor a taxonomy of transhistorical modes and functions. Instead, I focus on a specific esthetic practice that reveals within the acknowledged motivational grounds for the novel the basis for a complex revision of novelistic assumptions. Because this practice is exemplified in the trope of metaphor and thereby related to the study of generative principles in narrative, the thrust of my writing is speculative and eclectic. I draw on the overlapping disciplines of structuralism and poststructuralism, psychoanalysis and Marxism, using a theoretical framework that eludes both the restrictive esthetic categories of traditional genre study and the narrow conceptual scope of most conventional tropologies.

Nevertheless, this study does not elude the obligation of close reading. The central chapters of *A Metaphorics of Fiction* concentrate on textual densities in the work of three innovative twentieth-century novelists: Djuna Barnes, John Hawkes, and Samuel Beckett. The biases that inform my choice of tutor texts, however, are instrumentalist not monumentalist. I have not attempted in these chapters to authorize a new canon or to undertake invidious comparisons of classical and modern (or postmodern) texts. Such oppositional and totalizing strategies violate the spirit of this inquiry, committed as it is to examining familiar objects within unfamiliar frameworks, the better to comment perspicuously on the contingent nature of all framing devices. Indeed, if, as I argue, the practice of metaphor always entails a rigorous accounting for its own contingency, I am doubly constrained to a project that neither belies its own conditions of possibility nor takes stubborn refuge within the framework of its own enabling assumptions. As I hope my final chapter makes plain, this study does not seek a critical position to rest in but rather works to open still more laborious pathways of critical inquiry: specifically, a study of the relation between forms of subjectivity in ideology and literature.* What follows therefore is as much a prolegomenon to as it is a culmination of work that needs to be done in this area.

The ideas developed here germinated in the particularly stimulating intellectual climate of the English graduate program at the University of Washington. My fellow students Allen Dunn and Richard Katz were responsible for the spirit of intellectual camaraderie that makes efforts like this implicitly a communal affair and therefore especially worth doing. Professors Charles Altieri and Leroy Searle always convened a forum for ideas that was marked as much by intellectual generosity as it was by rigor. I owe additional thanks to Professor Donna Gerstenberger for her confidence in and understanding of the preliminary steps of this inquiry and no less for her vision as department chairperson.

At Temple University, I am indebted to the ongoing dialogue of the faculty Critical Colloquium, guided by George McFadden. My colleagues Tim Corrigan, Dan O'Hara, Susan Stewart, and Jane Tompkins all commented helpfully on various drafts. Nadia Kravchenko also deserves thanks for her swift, careful, and always genial typing of the manuscript.

At the Florida State University Press, Jeanne Ruppert, Helen Carroll, and Ellen Ashdown have given their support

---

*For an indication of what this work entails, particularly in relation to theories of the novel, see my essay "The Methods of Form: On Narrativity and Social Consciousness," to appear in *SubStance 41*.

and enthusiasm through every stage of the production of this volume.

Chapter 3 of this book appears in a somewhat shorter form in *Contemporary Literature*. The editors and the University of Wisconsin are to be thanked for permission to reprint.

Finally, I want to thank Nora Pomerantz, whose meticulous intelligence as an editor and whose patience and sympathy during the writing of this book sustained the effort to the end.

1
THE FICTIONS OF METAPHOR

The study of fiction has long teetered on the precarious distinction made between the genres of poetry and prose. Critical histories of the novel, which have guided canon formation, have thrived on the vaguely Coleridgean intuition that divides the organicist realm of poetry from the analytical, extrapolative, and therefore secondary realm of prose.[1] This dichotomy expresses the Romantic bias for form over theme and fathers the assumption that prose is too drably wedded to the particulars of objective reality to express a visionary consciousness. The considerable Romantic influence on literary criticism in general perhaps inspires the assumption of much traditionalist novel criticism that form in fiction is functionally subordinate to the themes of cultural life and the categorical imperatives implicit in them. Reduced in this way to Aristotle's *mythos* or story, the novel becomes mechanically unthinkable without the mediations of "reality" that in turn seem to give the genre a privileged standard of rationality. But this is precisely the position against which the polemical thrust of much modern and contemporary writing is directed; modern writing designates its conceptual nemesis in the novel's historical burden of reference. The rhetoric of contemporary fiction strenuously shifts the burden of reference from the conventions of the genre into the arena of philosophical skepticism where reference becomes

1

the object rather than the vehicle of the novel's formidable powers of comprehension.

The privilege of the referent has been the cornerstone of our institutional, scholarly readings of the novel genre. In Percy Lubbock's *The Craft of Fiction*, the critic imputes an unconditional causality to objective forms of life, in relation to which the rhetorical strategies of the text serve merely as a mode of adequation: "a subject wrought to [the] pitch of objectivity is given weight and compactness; it is like a piece of modelling, standing in clear space, casting its shadow. It is the most finished form that fiction can take."[2] Despite Lubbock's touting the formal uniqueness of the novel, the rhetorical presentation of subject in his view is structurally parasitic on the categories of referential reality.

Likewise, "rhetoric" in the title of Wayne Booth's influential genre study *The Rhetoric of Fiction* denotes a preformulated typology of narrative modes that have their foundation in the codes of orthodox humanist morality. Despite Booth's nascent metafictionist proviso that "whatever disguises the author of novels adopts he can never choose to disappear"[3] (that is, he can never escape his own rhetoricity), the author's appearance is nevertheless always circumscribed within habits of mind or a body of cultural presuppositions that remain unquestioned in their acknowledged eloquence. Even in Ralph Freedman's more self-consciously avant-garde updating of the canon, *The Lyrical Novel*, the assumption behind his claim that lyrical fiction exhibits "the paradoxical submersion of narrative in imagery and portraiture"[4] reasserts the dichotomy of a thematic realm of unconditional "objective" knowledge and a complementary subjectively conditioned knowledge of reality: the metaphorical "inside" and "outside" of post-Cartesian consciousness. The inside is typically accommodated to the outside as form is to content. In Freedman's own words, the general significance of the novel is therefore located "in the challenge of reconciling the 'inner' and 'outer' with each other and with the exigencies of art."[5] Even in works where linguistic density encroaches upon temporally plotted perspectives, critical judgments have been overwhelmingly conditioned by the reduction of form to a repertoire of already constituted subjective stances.

One methodological advantage given to the study of the novel by recent critical theory is its willingness to preempt the dualisms of theme and form, inside and outside, poetry and prose by subordinating the body of novelistic themes to the cognitive apparatus of rhetoric. For Paul de Man, a critic who has labored eloquently to place the discipline of rhetoric at the center of our discussions of the ontology of literary art, the prevailing critical dualisms that lead us into metaphysical pursuits of the referent, truth, reality, totality, etc., are best summarized in the opposition of grammatical and rhetorical models of intelligibility. The grammatical model denotes the realm of the referent and thereby reinstates the orthodoxy of inside and outside as a framework for analysis. But de Man is quick to stipulate that rhetoric for him is emphatically not one pole of an irresolvable (hence durable) dialectic. More precisely it designates the broad speculative field of tropes and figures that serves as the constitutive ground for all acts of mind. Rhetoric for de Man denotes an active reconstituting of the instrumental categories of language, not an indexical norm for language users. Therefore de Man asserts that rhetorical meaning does not depend on its opposition with grammatical meaning—rather it is the inherent structural principle of all literary meaning. *Allegories of Reading*, de Man's fullest statement of the rhetorical basis of language, is also his most emphatic statement:

> The grammatical model of [any] question [statement] becomes rhetorical not when we have on the one hand a literal meaning and on the other hand a figural meaning, but when it is impossible to decide by grammatical or other linguistic devices which of the two meanings (that can be entirely incompatible) prevails. . . . rhetoric radically suspends logic and opens up vertiginous possibilities of referential aberration.[6]

De Man opens a large and (for some) forbidding field of inquiry into the nature of literary discourse. He challenges the basic tenets of the humanist esthetic—authorial intention, formal totality, grammatical objectivity—founded as they are upon the dialectical structures of idealist philosophy. Consequently, the specter of a radical indeterminacy looms over the scene of rhetoric as de Man paints it, with more ominous portent than most *gentle readers* of "The Great Tradition" will gracefully accommodate. It is no surprise that de Man's detractors decry the prospect of a potent antihumanism in his relativistic account of literary invention, despite the fact that de Man's theory of language is emphatically echoed by the discourse of the modern-postmodern novel—where familiar elements of plot, character, setting, and theme claim only a kind of second-order significance as clues about the rhetorical devices that operate them. On the contrary, the antihumanism decried in recent critical theory must be confronted as already part of the humanist tradition in whose name it is condemned.

In view of the wide divergence between old and new perspectives, it is not surprising that contemporary students of the novel are finding themselves torn between conflicting but compelling critical positions. On the one hand, critics see the structural features of plot, character, and setting as organizing a thematic level of readerly interest that expresses the novel's historical and cultural contingency. On the other hand, the same critics see an inherent discontinuity or disjuncture between the formal devices that create representational presence in a text and the duplicities of language that constitute the medium of expression. Most recently, critics claim that this disjuncture calls attention to an authorial presence, thus validating a reflexive account of the *production* of meanings in texts; the *productivity* of the text is traced in the author's rhetorical subversions (linguistic innovations) of culturally sanctioned categories of intelligibility. These categories affirm the limits of our rationally constructed world within the strictures of conventional linguistic usage and hence constitute an obstacle to invention.

The metaphor of productivity or production is much used by critics who want to reconstruct the fundamental categories of literary experience by stressing the essential negativity of writing. This is a legacy of German idealist thought predicating the power of all conscious determination upon a negative will. The decisive connotations of productivity are therefore best evoked by setting it in opposition to the concept of *mimesis*, or imitation, the Aristotelian, pre-idealist criterion for critical judgment about narrative plot. Like de Man, who wants to reverse the usual priorities of referential and metaphorical value, avant-garde texts articulate meaning through self-reflexive rhetoric that makes the object of imitation—the world—less interesting than the subjective mind that can ever more scrupulously posit the world's objective existence. The text displays itself preeminently as process. Within the context of the avant-garde esthetic, productivity is therefore distinguished from the mimetic content of novels. The mimetic is held in comparative disrepute as a merely received—not created— commodity of culture. Since this notion of productivity implies a shift from discursive to rhetorical levels of expression, it is not surprising that both authors and critics identify it with metaphoric trope. For structuralist and poststructuralist theorists, driven as they are to account for the generative properties of literary language, metaphor is the essential mode of production. Metaphor exhibits the quintessential mediation of parts and wholes insofar as it is always a hybrid of mutually exclusive discursive contexts. And because it is an inherently self-reflexive trope, always disclosing an authorial presence, it is an apt figure for any discussion of literary self-consciousness. For these reasons, among others, this study will attempt to explain how a prototypically "poetic" trope guides the radical self-consciousness that is transforming a prose genre in this century. We will observe how a trope of classic rhetoric, which in simplest terms encompasses the contradiction of similarity within difference, establishes the most eloquent "pre-text" for modern novelists' brazen "de-familiarization" of reality, for their commitment to disruptive forms.

I

The productivity of the text is featured most notoriously in the deconstructionist ésthetic, recently proposed within the speculative tradition of French structuralist criticism by authors like Jacques Derrida, Julia Kristeva, Roland Barthes, and Jacques Lacan. Structuralist theorists insist that the novel's novelty must be explained by scrupulously confronting the presuppositions of its creative agency, not by hypostatizing the meaning of individual texts. Indeed, the structuralist project is conspicuously historical in its privileging of the enabling assumptions of a text over its formal structure. Although in this study I embrace the deconstructionist stance as a point of departure, I will also argue that the deconstructionist esthetic is most fruitful in the way it inhibits its own elucidations of the problematic it discloses. I do not wish to deconstruct texts but rather to capture the force of their respective conceptual projects through ideas made available by deconstruction. This means that I will resist the prevailing tide of deconstructions-to-infinity that is sweeping the contemporary critical scene. I will emphasize that we must be careful to preserve a distinction between critical and esthetic deconstructions. We must distinguish between the epistemological problems upon which deconstructionism thrives, for these are voluntary responses to the world, and the methodological imperatives that the novel imposes, for these are formal necessities. If we keep these distinctions in mind, we will see that while the forms of postmodernist fiction may not be conceivable without deconstructionist insights about the nature of language, the deconstructionist method alone cannot yield the fullest account of esthetic forms.

The promulgators of the deconstructionist esthetic naturally seize upon the domain of fiction because it is the literary form that presupposes a world view: fiction images a world. The project of Derridean deconstruction nourishes its skepticism on a cultural proclivity for such epistemological totalizations. Derrida sees this tendency as the foundation of Western thought; and upon it, insofar as it is instanced in the function of plot, the conventions of the classical novel also rest.

The concept of plot is doubly complicit with what Derrida attacks as a "metaphysics of presence," a metaphysics that assumes that language's ability to objectify its origin is evidence of its autonomy.[7] First, as the vehicle of a philosophically naive but historically significant version of novelistic *mimesis* (imitation of the world), plot purports to be a holistic disclosure of reality. Second, as the device of narrative closure, plot endows the formal autonomy of the text. In both cases, the question of how the authority of plot can be grounded is equivalent to Derrida's epistemological question: how can the subject ground its presence in the world without dissimulating its own otherness from the structure of meaning by which it attempts to express itself? Derrida proposes that the quest for "presence" must be replaced by an understanding of the desire structures that motivate it, even as he puts the relation of motive to act in dire question. The deconstructionist mentality never tires of exposing the hidden, destabilizing contingencies that Derrida would claim haunt every pretension to epistemological self-sufficiency:[8]

The signified concept is never present in itself, in an adequate presence that would refer only to itself. Every concept is necessarily and eventually described in a chain or a system, within which it refers to another and to other concepts, by the systematic play of difference. Such a play, then—difference—is no longer simply a concept, but the possibility of conceptuality.[9]

Derrida's wide-ranging attack on correspondence theories of truth—the claim that any signifier can display its own ade-

quacy to the signified that prompts it—jeopardizes the concept
of intentionality that secures the privileged status of authorship in the first place and thus demands a new account of the
production of meaning in texts. Indeed, if interrogated with
Derrida's own ironic fervor for subversive reasoning, the whole
framework of humanist values that attaches social, historical,
or ethical significance to the novel must humbly crumble. Derrida himself would explain that the conventions of fictional narrative remain inviolable in the popular imagination only because their pretext to refer to a world of lived experience has
not been sufficiently scrutinized; they have not yet been revealed as willful fictions. This is precisely the epistemological
naiveté that contemporary novelists appear (perhaps too eager-
ly) to shed. In the climate of Derridean skepticism, many self-
consciously "contemporary" theorists of the novel, such as
Jonathan Culler, insist that the prime act of criticism—by critics and by self-conscious novelists—must be criticism of embodied conventions, insofar as they claim epistemological "authority."[10] Projects like Ian Watt's account of the historical and
sociological conditioning of fiction and Wayne Booth's lexicon of
formal conventions are being abandoned as relative abstractions from the functional priorities of the text. Those fictions
now prominent in the emerging critical discourse do not use
existing models of intelligibility—embodied history, morality,
politics—to authorize the act of writing, but take the awareness of their own fictionality as the only legitimate impetus of
narrative. Within this context, some writers and critics now
proclaim the contemporary novel's unprecedented engagement
with forms of life, since for the first time the formal disposition of historical reality is conceived as a pure contingency of
consciousness.

   This engagement, however, is not to be confused with a
Sartrean *engagement* dictating the writer's responsibility to
the forms of his or her own cultural experience, for those forms
are only the disguises of a more fundamental human predicament. Deconstructionists argue that contrary to the teleologi-

cal certainties upon which the descriptive faculty of traditional
realistic narrative presumes, the reflexiveness of the contemporary novel offers an insight into the "fictionality of reality"
that is fundamental to all acts of mind. When the novel is aware
of its own contingency, it participates actively in the dynamic of
consciousness. In other words, acts of mind supplant the world
of actions as the proper scope for novelistic imagination. Paradoxically, realism is now put forth as a rationale of the genre
insofar as the genre expresses its own imaginative preroga-
tives as a threshold of self-conscious activity.

Critics seeking to legitimate the productivity of the text (the
self-conscious, self-critical use of language) as the novelistic
practice *par excellence* have coined the terms "metafiction" and
"surfiction." As Raymond Federman, a resident polemicist for
the *nouvelle critique* in English, stridently declaims, "To write
is to produce meaning and not reproduce a pre-existing meaning that supposedly precedes the words."[11] The metafictionist
theory, by decrying critical models for the novel that are bound
by expectations of thematic closure, claims to contextualize
better and therefore to explain more fully the stylistic idio-
syncrasies of modernist fiction—fractured plot, characterless
narrative, the self-referencing play of language—all of which
present world-disclosure as a vitally inconclusive process rather
than a formed product. The "fictions" of authors as varied as
James Joyce, John Barth, Vladimir Nabokov, Donald Barthelme, Jorge Luis Borges, and John Hawkes are dutifully invoked as works whose formal structures, by calling attention to
themselves as form, thwart a mimetic or representational rationale. In this way, such texts are contrasted with what Roland Barthes designates "the classical novel": the apparently
seamless continuity of esthetic form with the descriptive predicates of a specific cultural milieu.[12] The "classical novel," because it "comes from culture and does not break with it," appears
as a shameless tautology: it preempts the creative fulfillment of
writing by merely reflecting the predicates that license its own
expression. The metafictionists view this representational bur-

den as the soporific of the writer's self-awareness, inevitably placing him or her in bad faith with respect to the source and agency of narrative authority. Barthes particularly sees the implied confusion between the authorial act and the representability of the world as symptomatic of the narcissism of culture.

In *Writing Degree Zero*, Barthes traces the crisis of representation in the novel to the failure of the 1848 Revolution in Europe and the simultaneous ruin of liberal illusions. History, as Barthes reads it, admonished the bourgeois writer with the revelation that events no longer reflected the veracity of his or her language. If formerly the realism of literature depended on an equivalency of words and things, Barthes announces that "Writing is now to be served not by virtue of what it exists for but thanks to the work it has cost [the reader]," that is, by the opacity of the signifier.[13]

Barthes's pronouncements may indeed strike us initially as dogmatically a-historical and anti-cultural. But what appears in an early text like *Writing Degree Zero* to be a claim for a decentering and hence dehumanizing esthetic revolution is revealed in a later text like *S/Z* to be as much a legacy of critical history as an esthetic innovation. The prose artist's presumed break with culture then is revealed to be an intrinsically cultural phenomenon. In other words, for Barthes esthetic revolutions do not preclude or preempt history. Fittingly, Barthes's famous distinction between "writerly" and "readerly" texts (the one that comes from culture, the other that breaks with culture) finds its exemplary exposition in his reading of a paternalistically old-fashioned novel: Balzac's *Sarasine*. The limited plurality of the Balzac text is seen by Barthes to transcend, by means of the critical concept of connotation, the system of closure that operates its readerly codes. Simply, connotation is a process whereby a signifier serves as the signifier of something else. Barthes reminds us that the relative inconspicuousness of this concept in literary criticism is the result of its relative abstraction. Connotation does not lend itself to reification in a typology of texts. On the contrary, denotation has prevailed as the dominant predicate of critical activity because it lends itself readily to the preservation of a typology of texts conscripted to the standard of univocal meaning. Barthes sees the dominance of denotative value to be symptomatic of ideology insofar as its pretension to self-sufficient meaning is always a self-centering illusion, easily pierced by the ironies of temporality. It is on the basis of this critique that Barthes privileges connotation for the writerly writer and the literary critic alike.

But before Barthes's apparent reversal of the priorities of denotative and connotative meaning be construed as access to an unrestrained relativism, it is important to remember that in Barthes's definition connotation is above all determination— not an index of indeterminacy. Connotation is

> a relation, an anaphora, a feature which has the power to relate itself to anterior, ulterior or exterior mentions, to other sites of the text . . . one may say that it is an association made by the text-as-subject within its own system.[14]

Barthes's structuralism, his preference for connotation, does put the cultural order of the signified under interrogation, but the literary text is not as a result reduced to an absolutely subjectless drift of meaning as so many of Barthes's American epigones will attempt to persuade us. American practitioners of the surfictionist esthetic such as Ronald Sukenick flaunt the same renunciation of cultural "tyrannies" when they call for a style with "no plot, no story, no character, no chronological sequence, no verisimilitude . . . a style whose main qualities are abstraction, improvisation and opacity."[15] But the revolving door of such unstable oppositions as writing and culture may only supplant the narcissism of culture with the inverse narcissism of the text if the Barthesian critique of the signified is not understood within the need to clarify, not deny, a context of determinate textual and cultural forces. I believe that this is precisely where much recent American criticism loses the thread of purpose that originally linked French skepticism with the overthrow of conventional novelistic practices. This is where the metafictionist critique of novelistic convention breaks down, as the terms of its exposition become less clearly instrumental to its purpose. After all, even in Derrida this purpose is posited as a formidable critique of, not a vicarious flight from, culture.

David Lodge's recent work on the typology of modern literature is typical of the critical opprobrium concerning the metafictionist polemic. Lodge contemplates the prospect of a new literary canon of stories about writers writing stories in a *regressus ad infinitum* of authorial self-consciousness:

> If post-modernism really succeeds in expelling the idea of order . . . from modern writing then it would truly abolish itself, by destroying the norms against which we perceive its deviations. A foreground without a background inevitably becomes the background for something else. Postmodernism cannot rely upon the historical memory of modernist and anti-modernist writing for its background because it is essentially a rule-breaking kind of art and unless people are still trying to keep the rules there is no point in breaking them and so no interest in seeing them broken.[16]

Postmodernism, conceived as a continuation of the modernist critique of conventional mimetic art, is seen here to jeopardize its own purpose by reducing the impulse toward self-consciousness to an unconscious reflex of style. Lodge's intimations of anarchy are ironically consonant with the disruptive intent of conscientiously plotless, characterless fiction. But he is clearly less enthusiastic about the esthetic freedom these strategies proffer and more dubious about how they might promote meaningful statements about the world we live in.

And it is easy to appreciate Lodge's skepticism when the case against representation appears in a pragmatically detached rhetorical posture (that is, a call like Raymond Federman's for a "release from understanding" or an infinite deconstruction of authorial intentions) rather than in a true engagement with the specific linguistic resources that make representation (not to mention all rhetorical postures set against it) originally possible.[17] After all, representation is an expression of linguistic agency. To represent is to organize a structure for reflective activity. This conception is vital to the epistemology of Aristotle's *Poetics*, though literary criticism has been slow in acknowledging its relevance to the structures of the novel. In the texts of novel criticism, Aristotle's dependence upon the word "imitation" has often been perverted to the cause of the most banal realism. Later in this book, I will discuss the perverse naiveté of any understanding of *mimesis* as mere copy. For the moment, however, it is important to examine how the postmodernists' antirepresentational stance, "expelling the idea of order," does indeed threaten to "abolish itself," as Lodge says, but—and this is a crucial but—only if our descriptions of narrative discontinuities remain unattuned to the qualities of linguistic agency upon which all narrative practice initially presumes.

In his description of postmodern fiction as a "destruction of norms," Lodge cites texts that defy the expectation of a proper beginning, middle, and end; separate actions from the stabilizing consistency of character development; and fragment the linear pattern of plot actions. While Lodge's sense of the futility of such writing seems to be confirmed in the array of discontinuous "effects" he points out, the question remains whether some other descriptive means might be found to transcend the "effects" in themselves, and to comprehend the ground from which they spring.

Such a descriptive model is already implicit in the stylistic "deviations" of modern writing. Lodge's perception of discontinuous narrative as merely a rule-breaking art locked in a whirling dialectical dance with its opposite number is blind to the particular linguistic agency which grants such deviations self-consciousness and thus presents a purposive structure for our analysis. It is the self-conscious pose of such writing that, Lodge himself must admit, purports to justify the discontinuous style of narrative. This pose informs the metafictionist critique of representational narrative "presence" and spurs the revolt against it. The descriptive model that I will now propose in the trope of metaphor will help to elucidate the postmodern narrative epistemology without deflecting the problem of language into uncritical thematic categories. Though this trope is already an important topos for criticism attempting to define the intentions of postmodern writing (in the broad thematic terms of its revolt), we shall see that when this topos is specified beyond the vague intuitions of a thematic generalization and its mechanism as a transformational function of language is understood, it will help to illuminate the productive principle of all narrative invention. Finally, since I am interested in challenging the dominant modes of thematic naturalization, it is especially apt that I should take the trope of metaphor as the methodological lever of this study. Aristotle links metaphor with the faculty of genius: "it is the one thing that cannot be learnt from others." Insofar as it purports new meaning, metaphor always entails a radical suspension of the thematic grids that locate the threshold of meaningfulness in language and inscribe us in the familiar texts of our culture.

II

In "The Literature of Exhaustion," John Barth proposes that an awareness of the limits of originality becomes the threshold of unrestricted imaginative mobility in modern writing. The author cites the paradox of his own *oeuvre* as "novels which imitate the form of the novel by an author who imitates the role of an author."[18] The novel is conceived explicitly as "a metaphor for itself": it ironically displaces autonomous authorial vision through the devices that mediate its presentation. According to Barth, the implicit claim of "properly" intended novels to imitate action directly represses the knowledge that the conventional devices of their creation supplant such a claim. Paradoxically, it might be truer to say that it is the device that expresses itself through the author who uses it. Metaphor simply conceived (and more simply than will suffice for the ultimate purposes of this discussion) as expression of similarity is a perfect instrument for the self-consciousness that Barth credits to "serious" fiction because, in his view, the authorial act may be said to unveil itself only when it perceives the similarity between what it does and what enables it to do what it does.

At the same time, this unveiling entails a curious self-effacement. In other words, any employment of narrative devices that displays its own facticity in turn defers the self-rationalizing moment of formal closure, signals its own insufficiency to the real, and anticipates its own displacement by a more perspicuous, if no more conclusive, insight destined inevitably to follow.

The incompatibility of Barth's paradigm for authorial self-consciousness and the novel's formal proclivities toward epistemological closure may be clarified by the Derridean concept of *supplement*. Derrida asserts that any attempt to stabilize a field of inquiry by privileging an origin or center induces the instability of its own intrusion upon the field.[19] Within the field of language, to which the field of narrative devices is neatly assimilable, Derrida refutes the possibility for a totalizing comprehension on the grounds that the finitude of the linguistic system in no way circumscribes the potentially infinite redistribution of its elements:

> This field is in fact that of freeplay, that is to say, a field of infinite substitutions in the closure of a finite ensemble. This field permits these infinite substitutions only because it is finite, that is to say, because instead of being an inexhaustible field, as in the classical hypothesis . . . there is something missing from it: a center which arrests and founds the freeplay of substitutions.[20]

The principle of freeplay astutely comprehends the epistemological dilemma with which Barth's exemplary fictionist must struggle in his or her attempt to shed the delusion that novelistic intentions, the mere devices of the medium, create a self-sufficient ground of meaning. Correspondingly, I should point out that it is never a particular textual utterance, a specific array of formal elements, that interests Barth in "The Literature of Exhaustion," but rather what happens with every moment's realization that form itself is provisional, that is, the awareness of an infinite contingency of perspective. In fact, Barth's encomium to modern writing conspicuously avoids any pragmatic assessment of rhetorical density. Stylistic particularity is displaced by a concern for the idea of style. Barth praises the way in which modern novelists, their pretext of disclosing a unique purposive structure now utterly "exhausted" by tradition, use the conventional devices of narrative to "turn the artist's mode into a metaphor for his concerns," such as the circular structure of *Finnegans Wake*, the diary ending of *A Portrait of the Artist as a Young Man*.[21] Having said this, however, Barth has compromised the very esthetic ground of the enterprise that one assumes he, as a novelist, has been at pains to affirm.

Barth's dictum for the "exemplary fictionist"—that the writer's mode suffices as a metaphor for his or her concerns, thereby precluding a more fully determined relationship between linguistic form and authorial intention—threatens to make all but the most schematic readings of such work unnecessary. The text is reduced to its motives. What is at stake in the fictive strategies praised by Barth seems above all to be a metaphysical "idea" rather than an esthetic "form." That idea would be aptly illustrated, he suggests, if Beethoven's Sixth Symphony were composed today "by a composer quite aware of where we've been and who we are."[22] We would realize the ironic intent of the work as its chief reward since the automatic repetition of the form would appear as a category emptied of meaning. Such, Barth argues, is the reduction that our cultural history has already performed on the narrative techniques that constitute "novelistic" expectations.

But the more pertinent exposition of Barth's "metaphysical

idea" occurs in the literary exemplum that inspires his essay: premier fictionist Jorge Luis Borges's "Pierre Menard, Author of Don Quixote." In the oddly minimalist mode of this conceptually sprawling fiction, Borges's narrator relates the accomplishments of a turn-of-the-century symbolist poet, Pierre Menard, among whose posthumous papers is a manuscript of several chapters of *Don Quixote*—*Don Quixote*, but not Cervantes's. Menard's remarkable achievement is an original composition that, by a unique contrivance of fictive happenstance, "coincides" word for word and line for line with the work of the great sixteenth-century innovator. While Borges's narrative does not recreate *Quixote*, it generates sufficient commentary about such an enterprise that we must respect the idea of its doubling as the most eloquent commentary of all.

In Borges's "story," the similarity between the two Quixotes is the articulation of a difference that embraces them. That is, the authority of Borges's objective narrator is granted in a fastidious record of the contextual discrepancies by which he proliferates his own relationship with the single/double text:

> Equally vivid is the contrast in styles. The archaic style of Menard—in the last analysis a foreigner—suffers from a certain affectation. Not so that of his precursor who handles easily the ordinary Spanish of his time.[23]

Menard's *Quixote* tropes[24] Cervantes by obtruding a temporal disjuncture within the structure of coherent meaning that denotes the esthetic unity of that work. Thus, Cervantes's meaning comes to be ironically bound within the temporal perspective that separates him from Pierre Menard. Menard's reference to the "original" work (availed by this temporal disjuncture) in turn depends on the contingency of its own place within the more inclusive (hence temporally and historically disjunctive) narrative stance of Borges's narrator. Thus Borges's narrator gleans the significance of the temporal disparity between the two Quixotes much as a well-trained reader would tally a pattern of recurrent imagery unfolding against the backdrop of linear plot structure. The scholarly protocol of "differences" put forth in this way by Borges's learned narrator allegorizes the process of critical reading, ironically improvising a text of its own that claims priority over all others by its consummate troping of the trope.

Cervantes, then, the ostensible "cause" of Menard's *Quixote*, becomes an effect (a consequence of our readerly awareness of Menard) through the textualizing mobility of Borges's narrator, who establishes an independent authorial purposiveness in his every sifting of textual coordinates through the contextual screen of his own writing. Miming the distance of scholarly objectivity in his catalogue of Menard's literary effects, the narrator is repeating the repetition he records, immobilizing both Cervantes and Menard in the causal scheme of his own observing consciousness, re-presenting them under the aspect of his own commentary. In this reversal of historical cause and effect lies the tropological perspective that Barth hails and that for Borges seems to make of all texts the pretexts of other texts: metaphors for a textualizing activity that knows no textual bounds. In this case, what eludes adequate description— because of the lack of an ontological limit (an original text)— becomes accessible to discourse only by reenactment. Through an ever-evolving ontology of reading, the text becomes its own commentary, a metatext. Thus, in a distorted mirroring of Menard's doubling of Cervantes, we find Borges's narrator reproducing a catalogue of Menard's posthumous papers. This is his compensation for certain omissions in the original catalogue, the most notable among them being, of course, *Quixote*, which we can now by no means presume to have started it all.

"Textuality not texts" is the slogan of the deconstructionists, who posit authorship as an ever-receding horizon of intentionality, just as Cervantes appears as a diminishing point on the hallucinated horizon of Borges's story.[25] If intentionality is not accorded priority as the sole generative principle of a work, its teleological sway over narrative development becomes vul-

nerable to every conceivable misreading: an endless proliferation of new contexts through time. The deconstructionist *supplement*—the active ingredient of this interpretive stance—
challenges the Western predisposition to connect the meaning
of a text to a point of origin, to an author, to a specific cultural
and historical moment. To the Borgesian imagination, the mys-
tique of the "original text" must offer the clearest example
of this delusive logocentrism. Borges is certainly aware that
every beginning author's deference to appropriate beginning
devices betrays him or her to the dominant cultural predicates
embodied in them, predicates to which the concept of authorial
autonomy is thus paradoxically sacrificed. In other words, the
author's autonomy is made total and empty in a single stroke.

In the corridor of endlessly receding mirror images through
which one enters the labyrinth of Borgesian fiction, origin and
originality present themselves to Borges's reader as the *trompe
l'oeil* of a profound cultural narcissism that continuously seeks to
reflect to itself the image of its own desire. Thus, ordinary novels
—however well intended—serve the disclosure of a prior authority. Against the backdrop of this despair, the Borgesian
choice—literally to repeat rather than originate (write) a text
—proposes a more conscientious version of originality than
would be possible given the resources of any finite literary tradition. In its sweeping effacement of the authorial gesture
granted by culture, this doubling negates all those cultural values determined by the propriety of an original usage. While
this would seem to celebrate authorial freedom, the process of
textuality eclipses the isolated moment of the text. It follows,
then, that intentionality becomes an attribute of contextual relativity and disperses interpretation along the axis of a potentially infinite series of rereadings. Imitation in its turn becomes
a literal proposition for the first time, since the idea of representation of the world is supplanted by representation of the
forms of representation. And the forms of representation continuously return us as readers to the differences that our own
contextual circumstances make.

As Borges's narrator ponders the "originality" of Pierre Menard's *Quixote*, he leads himself into ecstatic speculations upon the conceptual novelties that must flow from the "new technique":

> Menard (perhaps without wishing to) has enriched by means of a new technique, the hesitating and rudimentary art of reading: the technique is one of deliberate anachronism and erroneous attributions. This technique with its infinite applications, urges us to run through the *Odyssey* as if it were written after the *Aeneid*. This technique would fill the dullest books with adventure. Would not the attributing of *The Imitation of Christ* to Louis Ferdinand Celine or James Joyce be a sufficient renovation of its tenuous spiritual counsels?[26]

The readers of Borges's "Pierre Menard" are privileged to a no less certain truth than those of Cervantes's *Quixote*. Truth, the epistemological threshold of the text, is now mobile across textual boundaries. The point we must not overlook, sharpened as it is by our awareness in this story that we are reading Pierre Menard without a text (only two sentences are quoted), is that the idea of the text is not anchored in the particulars of esthetic form. The texts that the narrator cites need no more compelling existence than the activity that names them here. Menard himself has provided a clue to this axiom in his decision to compose only two chapters of *Don Quixote*. John Barth makes his own point more explicitly in the judgment: "It would've been sufficient for Menard to have attributed the novel [*Quixote*] to himself, in order to have a new work of art from the intellectual point of view."[27] To speak of the text as a metaphor for itself as Barth has done (in order, among other reasons, to arrive at the judgment just recorded) is to defer indefinitely the propositional content of a discourse in favor of the differential play of contexts that points to its existence.

Barth's adoption of the topos of metaphor, with its sublimation of formal particulars, situates fictive invention between the Derridean poles of presence and absence, where the desire structures of authorship describe a familiar dialectical movement between work and world. In the case of the Borgesian fictionist, however, there is a difference. The author's struggle through his work to possess the world—that is, to resolve his own unsettling difference—paradoxically fulfills the longing for presence in a conscious proliferation of differences (stories within stories, texts within texts), which, by reaffirming the continuity of the struggle, metaphorically encompasses the poles of its dynamic. Under the pressure of this Borgesian epistemology, the author's representation of the world resolves the tension of his own incompleteness through a type of phenomenological reduction; the language of representation exposes the hidden structures of its own predication in lieu of the existential conditions that it ostensibly expresses. The author thereby suffers the inevitable displacement that the access to consciousness entails. The work of fiction is now usefully conceived as a metaphor because the referential possibilities of its discursive forms are presented under the aspect of self-conscious artifice. Explained rhetorically, however, this practice of self-consciousness conforms to a standard paradigm of ironic discourse wherein an author arouses skepticism about the sufficiency of his or her own statements or a text reveals its meaning through a calculated dissembling of formal autonomy. But Borges's and Barth's conception goes further; the forms of self-conscious narrative inspire a limitless irony, which subsists on the skepticism it engenders. This irony sustains a virtually permanent suspension of the cathartic *dénouement* that otherwise would resolve in the ironic displacement of readerly expectations to new and determinate contextual grounds.

Therefore, while Barth's use of metaphor as a critical topos deftly reveals the tension underlying authorial acts—struggling to declare themselves in a language that is never entirely their own—it does not account for the creation of particular meanings by which we recognize authorial acts to be authoritative. It does not sufficiently pierce the abstractions of a loosely thematic exposition that overshadows the form of the work. Furthermore, Barth's analysis does not account for the logical concessions that may be forced from an already "authoritative" language by the conceptual extortions of rhetoric. Instead, in Barth's criticism and in Borges's fiction, the "deconstructionist" presuppositions about the author's stance toward the world induce a perspectival regress that cannot stop itself, as esthetic form does, in the integrative capacities of its design. Within the warp of the deconstructionist perspective, forms reveal the pretext of their formal arrangement without preserving the qualities of that disposition toward formal arrangement that they seemed intended to articulate.

The epistemological instability of Borges's *ficciones* epitomizes the "rule-breaking" propensity of modern writing. Nevertheless, in its rejection of the contextual continuities by which we would more naively read *Quixote*, "Pierre Menard, Author of Don Quixote" fuels our skepticism about whether modern texts can keep their innovations within a discourse that appears always to be outstripped by them. Thus, deprived of our familiar readerly expectations, we are led by Barth's reading of Borges to the same impasse where Lodge decried the lack in modern texts of any stylistic rationale that might be adequate to the rhetorical density by which we first judged them to be problematic. We might now more perspicuously rephrase the incipient question in Lodge's dismay. How can modern texts disseminate their reflexive self-consciousness (Barth's metaphysical idea) in an esthetic form that does not discredit or supersede itself in the very process of its emergence? I will pursue this inquiry in the following chapter.

2
THE
METAPHORS
OF
FICTION

The theory of metaphor offers a structure for analyzing emergent meaning in literary texts. Metaphoric meaning arises from a transgression of contextual limits and thereby entails a reconstitution of the discursive ground from which it springs. Indeed, we have just seen how the trope of metaphor (itself a metaphor for the epistemological link between texts and ways of worldly knowledge) serves as an apt descriptive model for the ironic displacements structuring the metafictive worlds of authors like Barth and Borges. If we now focus on the conceptual mechanics of metaphor, we can see that it participates directly in those displacements by causing the self-critical stance of ironic negation to create new discursive levels.

I

By definition a transference of meaning across categorical boundaries, metaphor always moves through an ironic *aporia* by its obtrusion of an "improper" name within a seemingly closed semantic field.[1] Thus metaphor is understood, in accordance with Max Black's widely acknowledged "interaction theory," by assimilating contextual discrepancies so that they create a more inclusive, unifying context.[2] We might now say that Barth's explication of self-conscious fictions by the topos of metaphor actually confuses this integrative function of metaphor with the dispersive trope of irony, which is only a stage of its meaning. Barth's recourse to metaphor for the exposition of a theme of lost origin projects the meaning of the text outward toward epistemological relativity rather than pragmatically grasping the means of epistemological mobility within the discursive field of the text itself. Barth is interested in the negative rather than the productive properties of the trope. I risk another rehearsal of this metafictionist stance in order to disclose the one further irony that all its ironizing displacements ignore: the antirepresentational stance in modern fiction is characteristically an attempt to invalidate the claims for an ontological link between work and world. The metafictionists reject this link precisely because it is an unsatisfying abstraction, compromising the esthetic integrity of the work. According to the theorists of metafiction, to represent is to structure a verbal ensemble so that it is indicative of the laws that govern its articulations. In the words of Stephen Heath, what the text seeks to present is "the description of the conditions of the possibilities of sense . . . the description of its structuration."[3] The material density of the text is the relevant referent. Therefore, the metafictionists' resort to an abstract thematic rationale (that is, metaphor) for such structures is ironically complicit with the same critical naiveté that they dispute in their polemic. Thematic abstraction remains unattuned to the cognitive processes underlying the specific locutionary movements of texts. And in this sense the metafictionists' dependence on metaphor for a thematic gloss is incompatible with the reverence they express elsewhere for the untranscendable materiality of the text. It is with this understanding that I choose to concentrate on the mechanical function of metaphor vis-à-vis the metafictionist project, rather than to indulge empty metaphors for a metafictionist esthetic that seems to know no practical ground.

Production of meaning, not imitation, inspires the metafictionist, who, as John Barth suggested, conceives a new role for narrative at the limits of its traditional mimetic function—submitting the familiar forms of received knowledge to the hypothesis of new discursive motivations. The discursive continuities disjoined by metaphoric trope offer a ground for such productivity within the text. They are corollary to the background of fully determined cultural values upon which metafictive self-consciousness professes to work; in other words, the metafictionist author sees him- or herself as the reagent of a change in contextual meaning. Metaphor traces the limits of familiar semantic forms in its juxtaposition of disjunctive usages. Therefore, it is now possible for us to consider that the metafictionist reflex—supplanting culturally "centered" models of intelligibility—dovetails with the semantic productivity of tropological figure. The novelty of metaphor, its improvisational yoking of disparate contextual predicates, establishes the pretext of supplementing the language with a concept for which there is yet no adequate sign. Indeed, the concept of the renegade trope catachresis specifically endorses such an interpretation of the motives for figural discourse. The conspicuous otherness of the fictive worlds projected by modern novels might well be described as supplementary rather than hermeneutic with respect to the terms of human reality. In my next chapter, I will develop the postulate that a catachrestic style is in fact the catalyst of formal innovation in the modern novel. For the moment, it is enough to say that the live metaphor offers a model for fictive production—insofar as fiction is conceived as a rupture of the contextual seams binding established discourse.

Guided by these assumptions, we can expect to locate metaphoric meaning "outside" the existing discursive repertoire of a given cultural context. Correspondingly, as we have seen from the theory of metafiction, something very like the "outside" of fictive discourse appears in the suspension of epistemological closure, which renders the fiction of this century increasingly incompatible with the conventional expectations of readers.

To illustrate the effects of the foregoing theoretical considerations on a tradition of literary practice, I will cite an exem-

plary metaphor, one that might convincingly serve as a touchstone for the formal novelties of modern fiction; we can—for
the moment—call these forms modernist, postmodernist, or
merely experimental insofar as we are designating a rupture of
discursive continuities as an enabling presumption of the literary work.

Here is Stephen Dedalus, the protagonist of Joyce's *A Portrait of the Artist as a Young Man*. In the climactic fourth chapter of that book, he is undergoing one of those stock transformations of identity that typically unfold the dimensions of
verisimilitude in novelistic writing. The figure of a girl wading
at the shoreline serves as the vehicle of this metamorphosis:

> A girl stood before him in midstream, alone and still,
> gazing out to sea. She seemed like one whom magic had
> changed into the likeness of a strange and beautiful sea-
> bird. Her long slender bare legs were delicate as a crane's
> and pure save where an emerald trail of seaweed had fash-
> ioned itself as a sign upon the flesh. Her thighs, fuller and
> softhued as ivory, were bared almost to the hips where the
> white fringes of her drawers were like featherings of soft
> white down. Her slateblue skirts were kilted boldly about
> her waist and dovetailed behind her. Her bosom was a
> bird's soft and slight, slight and soft as the breast of some
> darkplumaged dove. But her long fair hair was girlish: and
> girlish and touched with the wonder of mortal beauty, her
> face.[4]

From a narrative perspective defined by strict linear expectations, this writing might appear to be perfectly obedient to
Aristotle's caveat in the *Poetics* that character is properly a facility of plot (*mythos*).[5] Under this exigency, the terms of character development are dictated by the *telos* of a cathartic *dénouement*. In relation to *dénouement*, all lesser transformations marking narrative progress to that climactic end are a
proleptic type. A reader may, on that account, reliably deduce

the logical proprieties of narrative. Joyce's own name for transformation—that is, the mind placing itself again in the tur-
bulent flux of experience— is epiphany: a quasi-sacramental
"sudden spiritual manifestation whether in the vulgarity of
speech or in a memorable phrase of the mind itself."[6] It could
be argued that here, too, the *telos* speaks loudly behind the
mask of classical dramatic revelation: a portent of the sufficiency of the moment to a temporal horizon of expectation. But
I am suggesting that, contrary to appearances, the "sudden
spiritual manifestation" of the bird-girl epiphany effectively
sets loose the structure of character from the coordinates of the
coherently plotted world of event, scene, and action rather
than representing the world that character, in its Forsterian
"roundness," typically denotes. In a novel of more discursive
means than Joyce's, representations might serve more scrupulously to objectify the wading girl as the contingency of some
further action. But here, all further action is problematic because the mind fleshed out by the figure of the girl is not
uniquely reducible to the circumstances motivating it. If our
anticipation of a plotted catharsis does not promise a likely reconciliation of the literal and figural imperatives of this passage,
then our analysis must postulate a narrative perspective within
which the divisive rhetoric will divulge its own rationale.

Joyce's own notebooks offer firm ground for such speculation.
The "Book of Epiphanies," professedly composed by Joyce to
lay bare the esthetic principles inherent in the ceaseless flux of
real-life situations, paradoxically supplies a motive for the style
of the bird-girl epiphany: displacing the "real life" (representational) situation with a figurative excursus.[7] In the epiphanies
of 1903–19 (these served as a forcing house for *Stephen Hero*
and *Portrait*), the catalyst for Joyce's luminous moments of
sight beyond the banality of vision is typically a detail obtruding upon a familiar context, not a contextual warp of significant
particulars. To the extent that the obtrusive descriptive feath-
erings of the girl on Sandymount Strand conform to this paradigm of recognition and revelation, the expressiveness of the

epiphany is intensified as a contextual lack. We register this lack when we see how the figurative embodiment of the girl surfeits the representational logic of the otherwise dominant plot situation. The metaphor of the bird surpasses the "world" projected by setting and action, which ordinarily condition the identity of character. Thus the metaphor appears to invalidate the contextual means by which scene and action may be unified in the purposiveness of character. I am now suggesting that the mediations of authorial presence provide an alternately viable contextualizing purpose.

The concept of character (in the most general sense, in which people are represented) has long harbored the referential pretext by which the language of novels is distinguished from the language of poetry. We hear the polemical ring of an enduring readerly tradition in Christopher Caudwell's interpretation of the novel as an explicit sublimation of language: "a work linking an outer reality [existence] with an inner reality [*mimesis*] by the already constituted forms of knowledge that validate expression."[8] In this view, plot may be perceived as an autonomous level of the text. It is independent of linguistic causes. Caudwell privileges plot, character, and setting over language as already constituted imperatives of formal identity in the novel. In fiction the threshold of language is only crossed by fully embodied cultural convention. Thus, in determining a theoretical basis for the contrast between novelistic and poetic writing, Caudwell insists that the "stuff" of the world crucially restricts the novelist's power over words: "This is why rhythm, preciousness and style are alien to the novel; why the novel translates so well, why novels are not composed of words. They are composed of scene, action, stuff, people, just as plays are."[9]

Within this horizon of expectations, the bird-girl epiphany presents a disruptive impropriety—a figural excursus that outstrips its own enabling principle: plot/character. The trope displays a figurative logic that does not restore the sense of a previous context under the livelier sign of another (in accord with the stipulations of Aristotle and Quintillian), but rather makes language the relevant context for its own activity. In Joyce's epiphany, the object of description is no longer a privileged region of interest. Rather, the descriptive attributes of the figurative sign overshadow the linguistic or imaginative contingency upon which all discursive contexts rest. This is the case for Joyce's bird-girl epiphany—as it must be whenever the figural mediation between contexts presents itself as linguistically overdetermined.

A good metaphor, Aristotle warns in the *Rhetoric*, "must not be farfetched."[10] Accordingly, the justness of the figure is determined by whether the metaphor's predicates may be shared across the boundaries of otherwise diverse semantic fields. The discursive movement, then, must always shift a reader's attention from a passive to an instrumental context, the latter conferring expressivity on the former. Nevertheless, this "transference" of meaning, while admittedly the operative principle of all classical trope, limits figurative discourse to a substitution of complementary semantic traits rather than allowing it to provide new meanings. The substitution of term for term that we find in many Aristotelian rhetorics reduces the practice of writing to a finite code of "acceptable" correspondences.

Modern theorists of metaphor—I. A. Richards, Max Black, Monroe Beardsley, and Paul Ricoeur—have questioned this rhetorical limit by proposing that figurative signification emerges within a dynamic "interaction" of terms: tenor and vehicle, focus and frame, primary and secondary subjects. This "tension" theory offers a meaning that is not taken from language as so many predicates unpacked from the lexicon of associated commonplaces (Black) but truly emerges from the frictional contact of interlocking semantic fields. Metaphor, in this view, constitutes a significant addition to language's repertoire of grammatical gestures. We can readily appreciate the need for such theories if we observe that while the Aristotelian transference theorem offers insight into the analogy between bird and girl, i cannot account for the excess of signification that the figurative "vehicle" carries. This excess is carried by an imagistic exten-

sion beyond the immediate contextual boundaries that originally warranted the figure. By comprehensively filling out the
descriptive particulars of the "vehicle," the bird-girl analogy is
redundant for the name-transference function (substitution
theory) of metaphor. Thus, the metaphor proves itself not only
the instrument of prior contextual determinations, but also an
augmentation of the cognitive grasp of experience that context
commands.

If, after Christopher Caudwell's example, however, we read
the words of a novel as purely adjunctive to an already determined set of rules, we implicitly consent to a protocol of literal
and figurative meanings, subordinating the latter to the former; the substitution theory consigns metaphor to an a priori
intention. In Joyce's epiphany, the bird-girl is at first intelligible insofar as she conforms to contextual norms on which any
linear progress must be based. But, insofar as the figure is
considered an extension of already determined predicates, its
purposiveness, in this sense, is always borrowed. Again, in the
Rhetoric we find support for this reasoning when Aristotle declares proportional metaphor (A:B : C:D) to be the most appeal-
ing trope. Its appeal is a clear subordination of figurative to literal meaning in a prescription teleologically bound by a fully
determined contextual scheme. This I will compare with the lit-
eralizing *telos* of novelistic plot.[11]

I have chosen to consider Joyce's epiphany in *Portrait*, however, because it offers an instance in which the figural movement of discourse, outflanking the plot *telos*, both disrupts and
affirms the continuity of literal meanings. In the bird-girl
epiphany, Joyce shifts the interpretive focus from the figure
on the strand to the authorial presence that so vigorously
clouds the immediate clarity of the object presented to Stephen's and the reader's view. The bird-girl epiphany subverts
the classical status of the metaphoric vehicle (conceived as an
extension of existent predicates) to a vehicle for authorial reflexiveness. Hence, the metaphor actively recalls the creative
basis for the contextual boundaries of interpretation, rather

than completing an already projected sequence of meanings. In addition to inspiring our wonder at her unexpected appearance and the potential offered for further dramatic unfoldings, the bird-girl incites our wonder at the linguistic markers that in her presence are a denial of the scenic (plot) context. The epiphany calls attention to itself as language and thus demands a more rigorous formalistic explanation.

Of course, only the most obdurate formalist would fail to point out at this stage of the analysis that the relevant character in the epiphany is not the girl but Stephen Dedalus, whose point of view the girl embodies. We cannot ignore the obvious fact that the transformation of the girl into a bird stirs the portent in Stephen's surname and as such enacts a dramatic projection of the character's flight of desire. Nevertheless, a further measure of the inadequacy of the substitution theorem is that it cannot explain how or why the rhetoric of Joyce's epiphany exceeds the characterization of Stephen's mind, which is the context that we are led to by a singleminded attention to scene and plot.

This understanding is possible and necessary insofar as the rhetorical extremity of the passage is distinct from the rhetoric voicing Stephen Dedalus's presence elsewhere in the narrative. The excess of signification carried by the metaphoric vehicle of the bird is distinctly marked as an effect of foregrounding, a concept defined originally by Czech theorist Jan Mukařovský as "the esthetically intentional distortion of linguistic components."[12] I have already suggested that such distortion alerts us to a contextualizing authority reducible neither to the mind of Joyce's character nor to the structure of the plot situation that deploys that mind as an organizing principle of the text. We begin to comprehend this authority only when we observe that the foregrounding effect of the extended trope (the epiphany) is clearly continuous with the rhetorical foregrounding that marks the omniscient narrator of Joyce's fiction. While the descriptive content of the epiphany (the image of the girl) is conceivably attributable to the consciousness of Stephen Dedalus, the rhetorical devices that set it forth are not completely assimilable to his character. It is precisely this *surplus* of signification that characterizes the prose style of the surrounding narrative context. We must examine the ground of this reference to appreciate the complexity of Joyce's technique:

> He was alone. He was unheeded, happy and near to the wild heart of life. He was alone and young and willful and wild hearted, alone amidst a waste of wild air and brackish waters and the seaharvest of shells and tangle and veiled grey sunlight and gayclad lightclad figures of children, girls and voices childish and girlish in the air.[13]

In this rhapsodic musical overture to the bird-girl epiphany, the conspicuous patterning of prose rhythms, consonance, and anaphora all anticipate a disharmonious discontinuity with the scenic predicates they invoke. In this passage, the attitude of romantic fervor that convincingly presages the spectacle of the girl on the strand is simultaneously mediated and thus distanced by the appearance of another scenic imperative: the scene of language. Correspondingly, and as though to confirm the force of this mediation, the image of the girl as bird appears to objectify and reify not only the longings of Stephen's soul but also the context of an omniscient narrative exercising linguistic control over it. The result is that Stephen's longing is placed within a field of language choices that denote an authorial presence. The obtrusion of this presence in effect repeats the emotional reverie that was at first attributable to Stephen on another level. But as repetition, it posits irony, disjoining the character Stephen Dedalus from the realm of assumptions within which the value of character as an organizing center may be contested. The concept of character becomes problematic: in the obtrusive rhetoric of Joyce's epiphany, Stephen's access of romantic feeling is granted a dimension of self-consciousness from which he is decisively excluded. The language of the epiphany, by foregrounding authorial agency, reveals the facticity of characterological emotions that would otherwise serve merely to authenticate the character's experience. The predicates that authorize the girl's transformation into a bird insufficiently account for the new metalinguistic context created in that transformation. This disjuncture allows a critique of Stephen's romantic projections on Sandymount Strand; it multiplies the possible interpretive strategies by which Stephen's thoughts may be made intelligible to a reader.

Where one context of significant meaning appears and another disappears in the bird-girl epiphany, we can distinguish between two practices: the substitution of interchangeable terms within a fixed contextual horizon and the full scale revision of the contextual parameters of discourse. The sliding of contextual boundaries is tantamount to a suspension of contextual closure, thus creating a contextual lack. In the dynamic of this lack, the productivity of the text is manifest. I shall elaborate this point in chapter four. In the manner in which the metaphor alters contextual markers of reading (that is, insists upon new predicative strategies rather than supplying new terms for old predicates), Joyce's epiphany may be said to offer a truly "emergent" meaning, a conspicuously "live" instance of metaphor. The category of the "live" metaphor is the jurisdiction of Paul Ricoeur's *The Rule of Metaphor*. Ricoeur identifies the metaphorical "twist" as a construal of contextual predicates at the limit of already lexicalized meanings, thus making possible a meaning that "is not taken from anywhere . . . a construction of the network of interactions that cause a certain context to be one that is real and unique. Accordingly metaphor is a semantic event that takes place where several semantic fields intersect. It is because of this construction that all the words taken together make sense."[14]

As in the decentering projects of metafiction, the productivity of a text like Joyce's epiphany is "measureable" insofar as predications that seem to be authoritatively determined can become radically provisional—and thus disposed toward specific new orderings of identity. In Joyce's novel, this provisionality does not imply an ironic regress of authorial self-consciousness as Derrida might have it but rather suggests the redistribution of predicative priorities across the rhetorical surfaces of the text. Instead of extending predicates (always ironically inadequate to the premise that invokes them), the epiphany extends the predicative practice itself to new structures of coherence, not to a horizon of indeterminacy. Where contextual imperatives are not exclusively determined, the text offers an epistemological mobility to the reader that transcends the restrictive choices of teleological plot.

Leo Bersani explains the metaphoric proliferation of Proustian narrative as the dissemination of the unified narrative self into a discontinuous array of diverse desiring strategies: "theoretically both the novel and the self are infinitely expandable."[15] It is this expansion of discursive possibilities that Joyce's epiphany also suggests. The novels I will consider in this study emerge from an esthetic that seeks to liberate the sense-making capacities of the genre from the narrowly teleological modes of thematic synthesis. For example, John Hawkes, in a telling counterpoint to the critical predisposition announced by Christopher Caudwell forty years ago, frequently insists that he began writing fiction (ten years after Caudwell's book appeared) "with the idea that plot, character, setting and theme are the enemies of the novel." Some of the most stylistically disruptive works of this century implicitly argue that thematic criticism haunts the house of fiction as it does because critics use this genre to mirror their own generalizing thematizing methods, thus obtruding the ghostly presence of a dead epistemology between the texts they read and their readers. On the contrary, the works I will discuss here conscientiously resist critical methods that are homologous with the dominant intellectual paradigms of their particular historical milieu. Inasmuch as such representational decoding systematically reduces textual differences, we may designate the fictions to be discussed here as, at least provisionally, antithematic works: their studied proliferation of differences as the ground of formal utterance requires a reader to qualify the naive inclusiveness of unifying predicates that might otherwise present themselves as closed systems. The modification of the substitution theorem compelled here by our rereading of the bird-girl epiphany parallels the revision of novelistic expectations proclaimed by many contemporary novelists. The substitution theorem is bound by much the same teleological principle that binds the conceptions of character and theme to the conventions of linear plot. The novelists who will illustrate my argument see the task of modern writing as an assault upon the ideological proclivities of narrowly teleological discourse.

II

We have seen how the impetus of the metafictionists—critics and writers alike—to resist conventional thematic closure often leads beyond the limits of esthetic form itself. Perhaps an understanding of metaphor as a constitutive agency will enable us to consider how the production of meaning may be reconciled with a concept of literary form. The project of metaphor, unlike much metafictionist rhetoric, does not reject *mimesis* but rather defines it under the pressure of a self-creating self-criticism that much contemporary fiction makes the burden of its activity.

Paul Ricoeur notes the paradoxical vacuity of all attempts to construe Aristotelian *mimesis* as the imitation of a world "already there."[16] In fact, *mimesis* is the inciting principle of tragedy, intended to express a human reality, not merely to echo a categorical imperative. This insight makes it possible to consider how the production of meaning may be formalized within a text as vital process. Ricoeur locates what he calls the "meaning event" (the self-production of the text) where a text suspends the ordinary completion of semantic sense secured by conventional contextual harmonies. With Joyce, for example, Ricoeur realizes that any attempt to ground an understanding of semantic innovation must wrest Aristotelian *mimesis* from the critical orthodoxy that "imitation" solicits an object or an objective state of affairs in the world. Since we have reassessed the function of metaphor in Joyce's narrative fiction, it is not surprising to find that in his notebooks of 1903 he comments on Aristotle's concept of imitation, anticipating the recent challenges to the theory of the novel. Joyce assents to Aristotle's "art imitates nature" with a qualification that performs its own metaphoric twist upon the most canonized precept of the *Poetics*:

> This passage is falsely rendered as art is an imitation of nature. Aristotle does not here define art; he says only art imitates nature and means that the artistic process is like the natural process.[17]

Art does not reproduce the forms of the world but rather participates in the production of new forms. Substantiating this claim out of the etymological roots of the word *mimesis*, Ricoeur reminds us that *mimesis* does not mean duplication of reality but imitation of human actions in a more noble form—that is, "poetically": "*mimesis* is *poesis* is fabrication, construction, creation." Hence, Ricoeur asserts that *mimesis* is the Greek word for an "unostensive reference of the literary work, or in other words the Greek name for world disclosure."[18] What is disclosed by the supervention of received meaning is the process by which the text unveils an ongoing production of meaning.

If it is agreed that metaphoric trope presents one idea under the sign of another, its semantic comprehension is always split between conflicting force fields. The capacity of metaphor to use this split to diversify interpretive stances may, in turn, offer new models of intelligibility to the traditional embodiments of the novel genre. I have alleged that while the metafictionists/deconstructionists expose the irony-prone reductiveness of F. R. Leavis's "great tradition"—the end-resolving *telos* of standard linear narrative—their own methods lead them to abstract their insights rather than capture them within enactments of language. On the contrary, the work of metaphor as it is taken up by diverse modern stylists now begins to account for the formal innovations of the genre preeminently in terms of language's capacity to generate new meanings.

Much as the austere formalism of the symbolist poets throws the full weight of context back upon the foundation of style—in order to resist extrapolation by external modes of understanding—content (the novel carries it as a heavier burden than any other genre) is often conceived by fiction writers now to be inseparable from the means that produce it. Agency is all. The avant-garde text thus becomes a form of self-analysis, possibly because authors perceive it as the only viable alternative to a discourse enslaved within the dominant representational modes of the culture.

Although contemporary theorists of the novel often leave the impression that the genre's "novelty" is a historical trait of the twentieth century, I will treat the accomplishments of the modern novel in this study as a significant innovation only insofar as they represent a revised methodological stance toward language (already implicit in the history of the genre) and not as they reflect the cultural changes that lead the novel into complicity with the facts of history. The burden of my analysis is to indicate how the rhetorical complexities outlined here turn the narrative eye of novelistic discourse inward to contemplate the springs of its own authority.[19] Indeed, many influential novelists of this century proclaim their enterprise now to be one of articulating what a novel is rather than what it is about. Yet the oscillation between these choices is not a new development in the genre. Any comprehensive historical reading of the genre will note the similarities between the reflexive self-consciousness of the twentieth-century novel and notorious earlier subversives of the genre—from *Tristram Shandy* to *Bleak House* to *Maldoror*. This argues against the radical originality of more recent work. Nevertheless, the focus of this study must finally settle on the stylistic innovations of modernism because, for the writers in this century, the theme of reflexive self-consciousness is radi-

calized to a structural imperative. As such, this theme demands
a revision of critical methods that Sterne, Dickens, and even
Lautremont never successfully commanded—their "strange"
books share a kind of pariah-hood in genre criticism, the unusual
turns of their prose more often ascribed to a psychological effect
than to an esthetic motive.

I have chosen Djuna Barnes's *Nightwood*, John Hawkes's
Second Skin, and Samuel Beckett's *How It Is* to limn this
study's theoretical perspective for two reasons. First, in all
of these works the novelists abandon the hegemony of literal
meaning, which legislates many of the discursive conventions
of the novel. This stylistic choice implicates the thematic level
of their fictions more deeply in the linguistic processes of the
text. Thus, these writers provide an opportunity to examine
the resources for coherence—beyond thematic reduction—that
are available to narrative. In this way, all three novels serve as
a pretext for speculation about what the novel is theoretically
as well as historically. Second, these novelists put the history of
the genre in a critical perspective by submitting the forms of
genre control to a reflexive rhetoric. *Nightwood* will illustrate
how the dramatization of competing textual codes can be em-
ployed by the novelist to qualify radically the controlling order
of plot conflicts and *dénouement*. It will show how agency replaces *telos* as the controlling interest of the experimental
writer. *Second Skin* extends the inquiry into the productive
agency of the novel by its use of the first-person narrator. Because *Second Skin* is an allegory of authorship, the first-person
narrative lends itself to exposition or dramatization of the
recursive logic of self-conscious fiction. Hawkes's novel therefore yields a rich perspective on the novelist's struggle to produce, within the devices of genre control, a meaning that is not
trapped by the narcissism of teleology, the tautology of conventional trope. Finally, *How It Is* reveals an assumption that
stands behind the characteristic practices of the other two authors: that a self-contesting rhetoric entails a significant revision of the category of the subject that underlies all our ex-

pressive acts. If these three novels are representative, they represent the attempts of theorists and authors alike to realize more fully the expressive potential of narrative acts.

Beyond their exemplification of an antiteleological narrative mode, the novelties of these texts can be seen as a significant revision of the paradigms of metaphoric logic. This is what makes them both new and wedded irrevocably to the past. Typically, *Nightwood*, *Second Skin*, and *How It Is* are all classified as "poetic" novels by critics wishing to forgive their infidelity to the "prosaic" lineaments of linear temporality. These texts are distinguished by their elaboration of metaphoric structures to a degree of self-sufficiency that vies with plot, character, and setting as the structural authorization of the genre. The disjuncture of contexts common to all metaphor—though usually simmering under the calm surface of reflected likenesses—now erupts in a destabilization of the balanced comparison (of tenor and vehicle). This brings about a further disruption of the literal-figurative hierarchy—implicit in tenor-vehicle—that otherwise permits a reader to subordinate the figurative sign to a literal context. Thus the reader preserves a semantic or contextual coherence according to the thematic conditioning of plot and character. By this means, criticism has long posited a dichotomy between the imaginary and real worlds of novels, the level of *mimesis* and the level of authorial comment. In the familiar novel of manners, the second term or vehicle often exhausts itself in an exegesis of the first term or tenor, the mimetic object that obtains priority as the proper end of discourse. For example, in *Middlemarch* the metaphors of dank cellars and clammy steps that echo their message of deathly reclusiveness in Casaubon's footsteps are completely assimilated into the structure of character. Casaubon becomes literally entombed in the cellared darkness of Lowick Abbey. In the realist text, metaphors are used up. The independence of the figurative sign to differentiate meaning according to its particular semantic characteristics is constrained within the simple didactic purpose of character development or literal exposition and becomes an excrescence of narrative progress: an "unreal," purely tutorial adjunct to the univocal references of the literal world. Contrastingly, the strategy of figuration in the novels I will discuss conserves the discursive properties of the second term (the figurative sign) in a sustained oscillation or "play" between it and its context.

It should, of course, be clear at this point that Richards's tenor-vehicle paradigm will be only a provisional construct of this analysis. Once his postulated literal-figurative hierarchy is upset by increasingly strained comparisons, we will be able to see, as in the Joyce epiphany, how the text *qua* writing asserts a reflexive textuality that undermines any simplistic notion of dichotomous narrative levels. When, as is often the case in the contemporary fiction I am considering, the vehicle usurps the contextual ground of the trope by proliferating itself, the univocality of the generating sign is lost in the multiplicity of its disseminations. It is thus denied the arbitrating authority of its literal or "representational" intent. Whereas the standard truthfulness of novels has long been based on words having a specific, causally related reference to actions they present, now the causal relationship itself is confounded by the obtrusion of the vehicle to a point where it purports to be a tenor. Thus, the vehicle is no longer comfortably assimilable within the scope of the originally prefigured (proper) tenor. Instead of nourishing the literal intentionality of the tenor, this vehicle declares its own purpose within the discourse. This "destabilized trope" more essentially "fictionalizes" its formal constituents by maintaining the differential movement between them—not as an irreducible difference but as the apprehension of simultaneously competing interpretive possibilities.

Here I might locate the points where my notion of dissemination of meaning via destabilized trope coincides with and diverges from the Derridean dissemination that served as a point of departure for my argument in the last chapter. My notion of destabilized trope takes its place in a literary tradition extending genealogically from the Renaissance tropology of catachresis: an abusive metaphor whose terms of resemblance strain the conceptual framework within which they are designated. The concept has its earliest exposition in Aristotle's curious admonition against strained comparison. It is a curious admonition because, if metaphor typically fills a gap in the conceptual repertoire of cultural languages, then the abusive trope would appear vital to the organic life of the language. Derrida, whose skepticism flourishes by putting a revitalizing strain on ordinary uses of language, appropriately designates catachresis as the archetrope of deconstruction. In "White Mythology,"[20] Derrida's important essay about the metaphor beating loudly at the heart of philosophy, his deconstruction of the substitution model of trope—he equates it with the nostalgia for the proper name, the token of self-present being—entails a reversal of the logical priorities usually assigned along the dual linguistic axes of semantics and syntax. The principle of resemblance governing metaphor in the Western cultural order privileges the category of the proper name (metaphor renames the object and is hence deemed improper) in accordance with the substitution theorem outlined earlier in this chapter. Metaphor functions in this scheme to redeem the lost presence of the name and thus renders syntactical distribution auxiliary to the purposes of literal reference, embodied in the act of naming.

By contrast, Derrida's attack on metaphysics depends on a more equivocal relation of name and metaphor. His most emphatic critique of self-presence, that is, the argument that meaning is always a ratio with difference and dissemination, finds its most vivid example in the syntactical modifications of semantic value effected by catachresis: catachresis, insofar as it is not predicated on resemblance, depends more upon the immediate contextual exigencies of utterance than upon a privileged semantic category within which a finite repertoire of terms may be substituted interchangeably. For this reason, Derrida contends that the word [metaphor] can only be in the plural. If there were only one possible metaphor (a dream at the basis of philosophy), if the play of metaphors could be reduced to a family circle or group of metaphors, that is to a "central," "fundamental," or "principal" metaphor, there would no longer be any true metaphor: there would only be the guarantee of reading the proper sense in a metaphor that was true. Now it is because the metaphorical comes into play in the plural that it does not escape syntax; and that it gives rise in philosophy too, to a text which is not exhausted by an account of its sense (a concept signified or a metaphorical tenor: a thesis), nor by the visible or invisible presence of its theme (the meaning and truth of being). But it is because the metaphorical does not reduce syntax but sets out in syntax its deviations that it carries itself away, can only be what it is by obliterating itself, endlessly constructs its own destruction.[21]

For reasons that are compatible with Derrida's subordination of semantics to syntax, I will ultimately argue that metaphor (Jakobson's semantic register) must inevitably verge on metonymy (Jakobson's syntactical register) insofar as the destabilized trope removes the categorical imperative of semantics as the functional basis of figuration. Syntactical distribution is primary. Nevertheless we must not fail to observe that Derrida's "syntax" in the quoted passage is functionally equivalent to the concept of *difference* and is for this reason ironically too metaphysical for the formalist orientation of my present project.

Syntax is Derrida's term for play. Because Derrida indicts a philosophical tradition bred out of the Platonist faith in determinate origins—an admittedly powerful framework of thought in the West—he must argue as if the privileging of the proper name is an inescapable point of departure for language users in actual practice. This is a highly doubtful assumption. In any case, the rhetorical practice that I have designated as the focus of this study emphatically does not depend upon such naive nominalism. Hence the emphasis of my analysis must fall not upon the explanatory power granted by the *concept* of dissemination as a critique of culture, but on the *agency* of dissemination—specifically the overdetermination of semantic values by syntactical agency—that situates the reader purposefully vis-à-vis the language of avant-garde texts. Because my interest in the destabilized trope implies a description of the formal imperatives of texts whose mode is dissemination, I am bound to illuminate the determinate practices of specific texts. Derrida is on the contrary bound to deny the existence of the text because it designates a locus of truth. Unlike Derrida my purpose in this book is to draw conclusions—specifically about the *kinds* rather than the *truthfulness* of knowledge made possible by destabilized trope. Above all mine is an inquiry into the uses of metaphor, in contrast to the Derridean project of ontological skepticism obsessed with the truthfulness of metaphor itself.[22]

Among other things my emphasis upon uses rather than truths makes it possible for me to assert that if metaphor successfully inaugurates new meanings rather than indexing the familiar lexical features of a discourse, then fiction no longer summons its significance out of an axiomatic opposition to fact, beside which it sits in restless subordination. Rather, fiction is identifiable with the act of mind that differentiates one discursive level from another as productive links of a new or emergent signifying order. Fiction therefore does not recapitulate to express, but hones its expressiveness on the *lapsus* of discourse. The esthetic values implicit in this epistemological stance court chaos. Such is the risk of any metaphor that erases the stabilizing horizon of linguistic norms. As a result, the disruptions that purge recognizable plot and character from the novel breed texts that are themselves like metaphors in their refusal to let concepts and images dissociate into complementary representations of physical and metaphysical knowledge, that is, the divisive thematics of realism and antirealism. The result is a literalization of the act of writing (that is, *écriture* in the vocabulary of Barthes, Derrida, et al.), renouncing the dream of its ultimate substantiation in a transparent use of language. Instead, the surface of language solidifies along the contour of displacements created where sense seems incomplete, the image opaque, the situational depths of the written scene sealed up. Narrative progress becomes an increment of distance away from rather than toward the cultural order of the signified. Everything is literal because the action of the text may not be grasped outside the composition of its incoherent moments.

Of course I am not alone in espousing the need of a rhetoric of emplotment strategies for the modern novel—a metaphorics of fiction—which will allow us to discover the ground of conceptual mobility that is otherwise disguised in authoritative texts by their formal correctness. The authority of conventional forms masks the contingencies of their linguistic power. Hayden White's *Metahistory* elucidates the master tropes determining the emplotment of discursive works such as histories, and White's insightful study sets an important precedent for discovering the "deep structures" of our most doctrinaire habits of story telling. For White, emplotment is "the way by which a sequence of events fashioned into a story is gradually revealed to be a story of a particular kind."[23] But whereas White is concerned with a taxonomic distribution of culturally prescribed functions of metaphor, metonymy, synecdoche, and irony, my emphasis is on the generative principle of trope in order to account for the motivational grounds of tropological practice. That is why my use of the word metaphor may at first appear eccentric or overspecialized. On the one hand, I agree with White's preference for the Renaissance philosophy of figuration, which does not stress the mutual exclusiveness of the four founding tropes of discourse. Contrasted with the more modern linguistic dualism that collapses synecdoche into metaphor and irony into metonymy, the Renaissance system permits a subtle overlapping of integrative and dispersive functions of language and, hence, a more flexible and fluent account

of literary styles. But my emphasis on the destabilized or catachrestic trope as a model for literary invention attempts to go
one step further toward a metafigural analysis. Metafigural
analysis transcends the literal-figural dichotomy that guides
most rhetorical analysis of discourse and that puts the study of
literary forms at a dangerous remove from history and other
discursive modes. For White, catachresis, because it inhibits a
literal/figural dualism, fights against the privileging of literature over other discursive forms and demands a more meticulous integration of the problems posed by literary texts with
the textual features of cultural experience in general. While
Hayden White does not ignore the place of catachresis in modern tropology, for him this trope is reducible to irony ("a mod-
estly absurd statement") and hence only expresses one of four
possible relations of the narrating subject to discursive contexts. On the contrary, in this work catachresis, understood as
a generative master-trope, is identifiable with the situation of
the subject itself—at least insofar as subjectivity, like catachrestic trope, is incommensurable with ("absurd" with respect
to) its conventional repertoire of narrative representations.
This is another reason why my study of modern styles will not
culminate in a new canon of texts. I am not interested in assert-
ing new criteria for judging the subjects of literary art but in
questioning what the creating subject inherently is.

3 THE HORSE WHO KNEW TOO MUCH

METAPHOR AND THE NARRATIVE OF DISCONTINUITY IN *NIGHTWOOD*

> I have a narrative but you will be hard pressed to find it.
> Dr. Matthew O'Connor,
> in Djuna Barnes, *Nightwood*

Perhaps Djuna Barnes's notoriously "difficult novel" *Nightwood*[1] has endured because it so typifies the by now canonical difficulties of modernist fiction: jumbled spatio-temporal order, minimal plot and character, exotic rhetoric. Joseph Frank, in his essay "Spatial Form in Modern Literature," is at once responsible for confirming *Nightwood*'s "importance" and sounding the keynote of its critical reputation:

> Writing of this order charged with symbolic overtones pierces through the cumbrous mass of naturalistic detail to express the essence of a character in an image; it is the antithesis to the reigning convention in the novel. . . . Miss Barnes abandons any pretensions to . . . verisimilitude, just as modern painters have abandoned any attempt at

47

naturalistic representation; and the result is a world as strange to the reader, at first sight, as the world of Cubism was to its spectators.[2]

Frank was attracted to *Nightwood* because it so clearly exemplified the problems that innovative modernist texts presented to a readership still guided by the rhetorical precedents of the nineteenth-century *roman*. *Nightwood* is difficult precisely because it does not respect the time continuum of the nineteenth-century plot paradigm. Frank essayed to read out of this difficulty the credo of a new esthetic and coined the spatial form metaphor. Nevertheless, as many of Frank's critics have pointed out, to supply a new nomenclature for the radical forms of modern texts is only to rename the problem rather than to revise the assumptions that forced us to recognize it as a problem in the first place.

Spatial form criticism fails to elucidate modernist texts because it merely substitutes space for time as the principle of coherence. Reversing perspectives, by shifting from time to space, is a simplistic procedure. Yet Frank's approach has an even more crucial failure in that he does not question the standards of coherence implicit in metaphor itself. The spatial form metaphor is particularly unilluminating for a fiction like *Nightwood* because Barnes's own metaphors are radically different from the tropes of linear-representational narrative. Barnes's figurative language insists upon ceaselessly revising perspectives, substituting one identity among differences for another in an infinite calculus of emergent meaning. In *Nightwood*, metaphor has to do with the act of predication or statement-making rather than the act of renaming that we identify with Aristotelian transference theories of metaphor. Barnes's insight into the source of metaphor's expressive power is the real obstacle to reconciling *Nightwood* with more traditional novels.

As I discussed in the last chapter, metaphor is, in the conventional novel, typically obedient to the well-known substitution theorem (a tradition of thought extending from Aristotle to

Richards and Black), which bases the expressiveness of the trope upon a field of "associated commonplaces." The "vehicle" may be substituted for a "proper" term precisely because it is already implicated in the field of associated commonplaces that the tenor denotes. In Barnes's prose, the balance between tenor and vehicle is upset. As I state in chapter two, with the term "destabilized trope" I will be referring to the asymmetrical relation between tenor and vehicle that I take to be the foundation of Barnes's style. Indeed, *Nightwood* will serve as a useful exemplum for the rather abstract claims of the previous chapter because, in this text, the substitution theorem is decisively supplanted by a rhetoric founded upon a principle of discontinuity rather than one of resemblance.

As we shall see, to understand this kind of rhetoric we should not look to the Aristotelian taxonomy of proper names but rather to the psychological structure of human desire that is Barnes's chosen theme in *Nightwood*. Recent psychoanalytical criticism locates the spring of human desire in structural discontinuities of discourse. For Jacques Lacan, the formation of the subject in discourse depends upon a paradoxical splitting (*spaltung*) of the subject from itself. The resolution of the Oedipal complex, synonymous in Lacan's work with the child's access to culture, language, the power of the signifier, entails a separation from the mother that is tantamount to an irremediable self-shattering. What the pre-Oedipal child (that is, child of the mirror phase, period of imaginary possession) desires in the person of the mother is the mother's desire, and to the extent that the child is identified with the mother, Lacan insists that he or she is not yet constituted as a subject. Lacan explains that the child is not individually situated or "registered in the symbolic circuits of exchange" because there is no difference between self and other. The child's access to subjectivity depends on the father's intervention in the pathways of the mother's desire. The "name of the father" deprives the child of the object of desire as the speech of the father divides the mother from the child's body (being). In this respect the father, who is by virtue of his intervention the representation of the law (that is, culture), impels the child toward the threshold of the other's language, where the child will discover the satisfaction of "having"—the signifier—in place of being.[3] The child's acquisition of the law (the word) whereby "having" is substituted for "being" leads to a quest for objects further and further removed from the original desire and thus inscribes the child in the linguistic code.

Language has been described by A. De Waelhens as a primal repression whereby "the subject withdraws from the immediacy of a lived experience by giving it a substitute" which will constitute the subject as subjectivity. Castrated, and removed from the mother, the child possesses itself now only through the relativization of the position of the other and the externalization of desire. Lacan's psychoanalysis engenders something like a rhetorical analysis of psychic process insofar as metaphoric trope is the model of the Oedipal succession to language. This is explained with lucidity by Anika Lemaire in one of the most complete expositions of Lacan to date:

> The subject is figured in symbolism by a stand-in or substitute whether we have to do with the personal pronoun "I" with the name that is given him, or with the denomination "son of." . . . The subject mediated by language is irremediably divided because it has been excluded from the symbolic chain at the very moment at which it becomes "represented" in it.[4]

The desire for self-expression, because it always defers to the coded other of language, entails a divided purposiveness that Lacan identifies with the productive capacities of metaphor. Inasmuch as metaphor adds a concept to language by restructuring the bounds of linguistic competence, it induces the instability of contextual grounds. For Lacan the act of substituting the name of the father for the satisfaction proferred in the body of the mother entails an instability of subjective consciousness. By extrapolation we might say that discourse proceeds beyond the narcissistic stage of closed meanings to more diverse relations of meaning when it involves a similar subversion of the narrating subject. In the present work we will see that Lacan's notion of metaphoric process (insofar as it arises from a radical displacement) echoes Djuna Barnes's refusal to reduce metaphor to the reproduction of preexisting meaning under a new name. In this way I will argue that in the texts of Lacan and Barnes alike metaphor is construable as the mode of alienation by which the self is bound to express itself.

It is not my intention to impose a Lacanian allegory on Barnes's fiction. In later chapters I will explore the implications of a rhetorical analysis of psychic process for a theory of avant-garde fiction.[5] Here I wish only to establish the methodological relevance of exploring gaps in contextual logic for new narrative potential, and thus to situate the rhetorical practice of Barnes's novel within the desire structures of the psychic life she wants to dramatize. As we shall see, the task of understanding Barnes's concept of narrative is not (as spatial form theory suggests) that of supplying a descriptive metaphor for the forms of knowledge it accords us, but that of describing the genesis of knowledge in metaphor itself.

I

The irrepressible question prompted by a first reading of *Nightwood* is: how is it to be a novel? The question is deliberately infinitive because Djuna Barnes's fiction everywhere gives the impression of a special case. It does not satisfy the traditional requirements of the genre. Here is a typical example of descriptive detail that acutely subtends the straight line of narrative:

In her face was the tense expression of an organism surviving in an alien element. She seemed to have a skin that was the pattern of her costume: a bodice of lozenges, red and yellow, low in the back and ruffled over and under the

arms, faded with the reek of her three-a-day control, red
tights, laced boots—one somehow felt they ran through
her as the design runs through hard holiday candies, and
the bulge in the groin where she took the bar, one foot
caught in the flex of the calf, was as solid, specialized and
as polished as oak. The stuff of the tights was no longer a
covering, it was herself; the span of the tightly stitched
crotch was so much her own flesh that she was as unsexed
as a doll. The needle that had made one the property of the
child made the other the property of no man. (13)

While *Nightwood* evokes the familiar conventions—plot,
character, setting, theme—they are submitted, in the course of
reading this text, to a decidedly unnovelistic rhetorical perspective: they are dramatically mediated by the play of language. After the first page of *Nightwood*, it is clear to a reader
that the familiar structural devices of the genre must be decisively reinterpreted. By attending to what I have called the
"productivity" of the text, that is, its way of restructuring interpretive paradigms, criticism will find its most rewarding
focus in *Nightwood*.

In his influential preface to the first American edition of
Nightwood, T. S. Eliot implied that the term *novel* had perhaps become too debased to apply to a prose work whose principles of coherence diverged so widely from the path of its
predecessors:

> most contemporary novels are not really "written." They
> obtain what reality they have largely from an accurate ren-
> dering of the noises that human beings currently make in
> their daily simple needs of communication; and what part
> of a novel is not composed of these noises consists of a
> prose which is no more alive than that of a competent
> newspaper writer or governmental official. A prose that is
> altogether alive demands something of the reader that the
> ordinary novel-reader is not prepared to give. (xii)

Evident in Eliot's reluctance to apply generic conventions in evaluating Barnes's prose is a radically subversive insight: language itself implies a conceptual freedom that the genre may acknowledge only at the risk of a devastating irony. In this view, language experiments and the novel may well appear to be irreconcilably at odds with each other. After all, the novel conceived by George Eliot as a "faithful account of the men and things as they have mirrored themselves in my mind" owes its formal articulation to a successful sublimation of language: a reduction of the variety of emergent meanings to a finite repertoire of expressive choices circumscribed within acceptable social practice. In the conventional novel, every attempt to exploit the inherent duplicities of language threatens the coherence of statements that flow from it.

Writing elsewhere of Joyce's *Ulysses*, T. S. Eliot questioned the standard of intelligibility imposed by the social nature of generic categories. In response to claims that the luxurious play of Joyce's language overwhelms the sense-making categories of the genre, Eliot wrote: "If [*Ulysses*] is not a novel, that is simply because the novel, instead of being a form, was simply the expression of an age which had not sufficiently lost all form to feel the need of something stricter."[6] It is frequently said that Joyce acknowledges the basis for an authorial self-consciousness that would reground the genre, making its status within language a contingency of its expression. Perhaps what is "stricter," in Eliot's phrase, than the assumption of canonical forms is a realization of the contingency of desire that form suppresses. By reaffirming the subject's mobility within the finite linguistic code, perhaps the novel can elude the ideological ends toward which its formal principles are frequently disposed. Our understanding of form, then, is pressed toward the condition of act so that we may now link it explicitly with a notion of emergent meaning. This will be to return the novel to the creative agency of all fictive intent.

If we now attempt to answer the question, How is *Nightwood* to be a novel?, we can begin by seeking a new kind of coherence amidst the radical dispersal of orthodox codes conferring novelistic propriety. In *Nightwood*, the psychology of the lie (all of Barnes's characters are liars) provides a useful context for anatomizing this tension between conventionalized forms of meaning and meaning emergent from an insight into the contingency of form. Of course, the notion of form I am provisionally adopting here accords with Aristotle's teleological pattern bound by a doctrine of final cause. But the duplicity of the lie intrinsically jeopardizes this concept of form by its implementation of a split *telos*. The lying consciousness knows two contradictory purposes. This split is integral to the problem of reading *Nightwood* because it has a stylistic corollary in Djuna Barnes's deployment of metaphoric trope. Barnes's metaphors "split" the contextual force field in which they emerge by the strategy of elaborate imaginistic digression such as we have just seen in the description of the circus performer. In this way we might say metaphor is the form-giving distortion of novelistic form in *Nightwood*. It marks the incursion of poetry into the domain of prose. For these reasons I will argue that the destabilized or extended trope is at odds with all the reductive unities of teleological plot. When plot comes into question so do character and theme. By this seemingly circuitous route Barnes's novel brings us to a profound speculation on the expressive possibilities of the genre.

Indeed we cannot separate the rhetoric of the lie from Barnes's notion of character. Fate looms for her characters in the inevitability of unrequited love. Honest desire seems to preclude possession of the loved object. So in *Nightwood* the lie is the lover's contraband. It is the possession of the other in the usurpation of the other's place. The lie denies the fixity of any relationship that would bind the subject to a hypostatized "truth." The lie frees the imagination to reconceive the object of its desire in order to implicate it more profoundly in the processes of the desiring self. The figure whose negation sustains the other characters' desire is Robin Vote. In Robin, as in the lie, teleological purpose is suspended, making radically contingent—hence wholly unsatisfactory—every attempt on the part of other characters to know (love) her. Robin must be denied by her lovers because she is inaccessible to them. She cannot be assimilated to the expectations that structure their relationship to her.

Yet, perversely, their denial is the ritual of a courtship, since they extract a solacing emotion from their deepening involvement with their own frustrations. As one character, pressed in the tormenting embrace of this paradox, explains: "I thought I loved her [Robin] for herself but I found out it was for me." Desire is tragically experienced by Barnes's characters as a crushingly narcissistic isolation. Because the reader stands in much the same relation to the novel as do the characters to Robin, their example may be utilized to construe a perspective that transcends the melodrama of thwarted passion. In doing so, the reader may elude the restraints of a banal thematic logic. By discovering the ways in which the reader's analogous predicament demands a restructuring of interpretive conventions, we can perhaps legitimize a reading of *Nightwood* that escapes the tragic psychology immobilizing Barnes's characters.

The tradition of the Anglo-American novel, indebted as it is to the genealogical transmission of narrative plot, bases the development of character on a fathering seed of personality. In *A Future for Astyanax*, Leo Bersani analyzes the tension between what he calls characterological desire and models of personality that privilege unitary coherence. The imaginative freedom of multiplicity is typically sacrificed to the stabilizing unity of the Freudian ego. Bersani claims that the very susceptibility of literary characters to such psychoanalytic interpretation reflects the triviality of their desires: "Everything which characters say and do can now be traced back to a determining structure from the past which impoverishes present behavior by making it both tautological and excessively coherent."[7]

Robin Vote offers an example of a character whose resistance to an analysis of psychological depth fosters just the multiplicity of interpretive strategies that Bersani would credit to a text's originality. Even more important for my attempt to understand the productivity of this text in particular and hence the terms of its novelhood, Barnes's characterization of Robin Vote presents a striking analogy with the structure of metaphor. Indeed, my claims about the inherent rhetorical character of fiction are dramatized in the elaborately figured prose that introduces Robin in *Nightwood*:

> The perfume that her body exhaled was of the quality of that earth-flesh, fungi which smells of captured dampness and yet is so dry and overcast with the odor of oil of amber which is an inner malady of the sea, making her seem as if she had invaded sleep incautious and entire. Her flesh was the texture of plant life, and beneath it one sensed a frame broad, porous, and sleep-worn as if sleep were a decay fishing her beneath a visible surface. Above her head was an effulgence as of phosphorous glowing about the circumference of a body of water—as if her life lay through her in the ungainly luminous deteriorations—the troubling structure of the born somnambule, who lives in two worlds— meet of child and desperado. (34–35)

> The woman who presents herself as a "picture" forever arranged is, for the contemplative mind, the chiefest danger. Sometimes one meets a woman who is beast turning human. Such a person's every moment will reduce to an image of a forgotten experience: a mirage of an eternal wedding cast on the racial memory; as insupportable a joy as would be the vision of an eland coming down an aisle of trees, chapleted with orange blossoms and bridal veil, a hoof raised in the economy of fear stepping in the trepidation of the flesh that will become myth; as the unicorn is neither man nor beast deprived but human hunger pressing its breast to its prey. (37)

The verbal exorbitance of this writing clearly precludes any easy acknowledgment of a limiting context and in this way announces *Nightwood*'s break with traditional narrative. The imagistic development of these paragraphs is radically disjunctive with the descriptive endowments of "white flannel trousers," "lacquered pumps," and "long beautiful hands" which dress up the illusion of a reclining, sleep-buoyed woman of Paris in the immediately preceding passage. Here the expository function of plot is supplanted with a practice of linguistic foregrounding. Instead of forming consistent expectations about character, the precipitous elaboration of metaphor divests contextual markers of their mediating power by throwing into question their continuity with the rest of the text. Indeed, Barnes's strategy seems explicitly to deny the substitution theorem of metaphor, which explicates trope as an extension of established predicates and thus consigns it to the status of a commentary.[8] In fact, this passage reflects the inherent instability of the component elements of metaphor (tenor and vehicle) that in a more conventional novel balance figurative and literal levels of representation, achieving a contextually harmonious closure.

The interpretive difficulty posed by the dense rhetoric introducing Robin (in addition to its complicity in the other characters' misunderstanding) is profoundly implicated in the psychology/esthetic of the lie. We take it as a given that the lie effectively dramatizes the problem of knowing by its ordination of a split plot *telos*. But in *Nightwood* the lie extends the terms of this "problem" into an esthetic practice wherever literal representation (and hence the thematic power of representational narrative to grasp knowledge by a univocal principle) is seemingly betrayed to the ambiguity of a figurative sign. Obviously, the force of these lies falls outside the precincts of moral judgment and so demands a new understanding. For just as the lie that Robin gives to those characters presuming to know her has no correlate and stabilizing truth (we never know definitely who Robin is and what her motives are), so the literal-figurative dualism that reigns over conventional novels is denied its mediating authority in *Nightwood*. For example, in the first quoted paragraph, the metaphors of earth, oil of amber, and decay do not refer back to an authenticating context harboring the secret truth of Robin's character.

In the rhetorics of the English Renaissance, the classification of a trope that strayed beyond the field of contextual determinations warranting its usage was catachresis. This term Jacques Derrida has recently co-opted to his deconstructionist project, refocusing it as "the use of a sign by violence, force of abuse with the imposition of a sign on a sense not yet having a proper sign in the language."[9] In keeping with the objectives of my analysis of destabilized trope, I want to point out that there is no simple substitution of terms, no contextual reflexivity in catachrestic discourse.[10] Rather, it is precisely the anteriority of catachresis to the devices of contextual closure that, for Derrida, fulfills its usefulness to philosophy and, for the purposes of this study, makes it instructive for an understanding of the rhetorical density of fiction.

Derrida acquires his understanding of catachresis from Pierre Fontanier's *Figures du Discours* (1830), one of the last treatises of rhetoric prior to its dissolution as a discipline of formal learning in the nineteenth century. In fact, the concept of catachresis must have particular resonance for Derrida because Fontanier's own exposition of the "renegade trope" is designated as a "supplement to the theory of tropes." Like the concept of *supplement* he presented in "Structure, Sign, and Play," designating both an addition to an existing frame of reference and its reconstitution, Derrida points out that catachresis does not present its meaning outside language but rather transforms the functioning of language itself: "it produces with the same material, new rules of exchange, new meanings."[11]

The call for "new rules of exchange" is answered by the transformational character of Djuna Barnes's metaphoric prose as well as by the radical transformations to which the characters of this novel succumb as they adjust to Robin's nature. But the clearest indication that the concept of character itself is altered by a catachrestic perspective and that the linguistic processes of the text must bear an unusual weight of interpretive attention is conveyed in the character of Dr. Matthew "Mighty

Grain of Salt" O'Connor. Paradoxically charged with the novelistic burden of explaining Robin Vote to all the other characters, he employs the same strategy of metaphoric displacement
with which I have identified the omniscient narrative voice of
Nightwood. Dr. O'Connor, the Tiresian oracle of human dis-
appointments, produces an echo of Barnes's own locutionary
movements, which an attentive reader cannot fail to hear:

> The darkness is the closet in which your lover roosts her
> heart and that nightfowl that caws against her spirit and
> yours dropping between you and her the awful estrange-
> ment of his bowels. (89)

Here, as in the metaphor projecting Robin Vote's trance of
decay, Dr. O'Connor's strategy extends the metaphoric vehicle
beyond the scope of predications that authorize his own speaking. On the one hand it seems paradoxical that the most fully
"characterized" voice in *Nightwood* is the most indistinguishable from the authorial presence. But on the other hand, this is
a defining feature of the dilemma upon which the plot (such as it
is) of this novel is founded.

The desire to possess an other (dramatized here by Robin's
husband, Felix Volkbein, and her lovers, Nora Flood and Jenny
Petherbridge) is probably nowhere more pronounced as a feature of the novelistic text than in characterization—in an author's own desire to present character as the objective embodiment of an independent will. In *Nightwood,* however, the
authorial gesture toward characterization, toward the other,
entails an interesting confusion about the authorial self and a
broadened consideration of the discursive properties of the
work. We have seen in the sinister homily of darkness, typical
of the doctor's pontificatory idiom, that what links the author's
and character's voices here is a predilection for epigrammatic
statement. Miming the duplicitous teleology of the lie, the pronouncements of the narrator and the doctor almost always ar-
range themselves paratactically as pairs of literal-discursive
and figural-extrapolative complements. "Love becomes the de-

posit of the heart, analogous in all degrees to the 'findings' in a tomb" (56) declaims the omniscient narrator about Nora's love for Robin. What follows is an elaboration of the entombment figure to a contextual extremity: "As in one will be charted the taken place of the body the raiment, the utensils necessary to its other life, so in the heart of the lover will be traced an indelible shadow, that which he loves." Typically in Barnes's prose the contextual cue that invokes the figurative analogy is transformed into a contingency of its extension. What appears to be the logic of the literal expression is nullified by a countercurrent of figurative detail.

The extension of this stylistic practice to Dr. O'Connor points up a more diffuse but more pervasive figurative pattern emerging in *Nightwood* as this character becomes a vehicle for transcending the opposition narrator/character along the very lines that the destabilized trope transcends the literal/figurative dichotomy. Contrary to the Forsterian precept that "rounded" characters bring the novel "to life," the more Dr. O'Connor's character is filled out by habits of speech that echo the omniscient narration, the more he is betrayed to the terms of his facticity, the pretense of art, the immanence of authorial will. Moreover, while the attempt of other characters to possess Robin is abortive, the author's inverse failure to draw a "realistic" free-standing character is reflexively self-productive. This productivity, however, entails a reassessment of the threshold of the text's formal integrity. The doctor's manner of speech produces, in tandem with the omniscient narrator of *Nightwood*, a coherent linguistic practice. Rather than filling out the particulars of character, this linguistic practice ultimately forces us to reconceive the category of character as an aspect of authorial presence.

II

I have noted the subordinate status that substitutive metaphors possess in more traditional narratives. In most, the referential level automatically takes precedence over the figural level insofar as it sets in motion the systems of plot, character, setting, etc., organizing hierarchies of relatedness in accordance with standards of verisimilitude. By comparison with the standard of verisimilitude, "figure"—which in the famous Aristotelian formulation ideally works to "enliven" the familiar—is quixotic, ephemeral, nonessential, and supplementary.[12] How can it sustain the coherent patterns of correspondent act and image that propel dramatic momentum? The predominantly figurative mode of *Nightwood* would consequently appear unsuited to the most banal referential pretexts of this genre pattern. The circuit of reference is decisively broken in the rhetoric of Dr. O'Connor and the omniscient narrative voice. Each additional gesture of metaphoric elaboration has the effect of seemingly dispersing rather than integrating the elements of a coherent pattern.

As I have said, the distinguishing feature of Barnes's technique in *Nightwood* is vividly displayed in the metaphor of the eland (quoted earlier), which abstracted Robin Vote to a contextual field remote from the scene and action that ostensibly motivated it. That figure reached its contextual extremity in a homiletic formula: "as the unicorn is neither man nor beast deprived but human hunger pressing its breast to its prey." The unicorn, the mythic animal, is "the meet" of the desiring subject and a world that is always insufficient to its imaginary needs, hence a world always mauled in its embrace. The homily marks the "extremity" of the figure because it does not explicate its own connection with the surrounding context. We might say that the doctor's homily projects the scene's meaning toward a yet unrevealed contextual ground within which its immediate abstraction could be clarified.

The image is traditionally meaningful in dramatic literature as it expresses the "inner necessity" of the plot teleology. By contrast, the image of the eland presents a contextual impertinence because it seems *un*necessary in these terms. While the necessity to which the eland is bound may not be immediately evident by virtue of its juxtaposition with the unicorn and Robin Vote, it nevertheless does anticipate the doctor's monologue one hundred pages later when he conveys his impression of Robin's beauty to Nora. Of Robin's childish face he exclaims: "The temples [are] like those of young beasts cutting horns as if they were sleeping eyes" (134). Here in the last chapter of his monologue, the doctor nourishes Nora's human hunger for a love that is inseparable from her own desire. He simultaneously offers sustenance to the reader's desire for formal coherence, for a continuity of purpose. For the temples of the young beast in the seventh chapter of *Nightwood* recall the "unicorn," the metaphor of the beast turning human (indeed, the beast *created* by the human) which endowed Robin's character in the second chapter. Like the metaphor of the eland and the unicorn, the figure of the young beasts cutting horns marks in its imagistic abstraction an abridgement of the immediate dramatic context. But rather than dissolving contextual logic, it offers a new grid of logical coordinates. The emergence of contextual links between the passage that introduced Robin and the doctor's recollection of young beasts reveals a new discursive level that does not appear to be bound by the Kantian "final purpose" that conditions our sense of closure and form. For this reason, I wish to equate it with what Paul Ricoeur (after Roman Jakobson) designates as a "second order reference," an indirect reference built upon the foundation of a more direct reference.[13]

It is by virtue of a second-order structure of meaning that the doctor's disjunctive patterns gain intelligibility outside the direct reference of plot and character, though they remain fairly enigmatic within those structures. For example, the young beast cutting horns extends the bestial imagery from the earlier passage, but quite clearly not as an elaboration of Robin's character. Rather, it is a way of expanding the image of the horn to new associative possibilities. The horn in the case of the unicorn expressed the imaginative deformation of human desire. Here it is linked to the eye not as the instrument of physical blindness, but as the metaphoric product of its sleep. Only the spiritually blind would equate sleep with deprivation of experience. For sleep, the activity of the night, produces the unicorn to satisfy human desires. It is this horn of the imagination upon which the "other" is always impaled. So the dream of that sleep and the hunger of imagination pressing its breast to its prey in the night (which is the metaphoric umbrella for all of these images) coalesce in the doctor's bestial characterization of Robin. But this is not the simple crystallization of an image pattern across the threshold of different contexts that we find in more conventional novels. The "pattern" denoted by the recurrent imagery of the horn and the human beast is above all indicative of a "practice" of narrative digression and supplementation whereby the expressiveness of the image comes to depend on its proliferation of new relational possibilities. Indeed, once we have been cued to the cross-referencing of the eland with the beasts cutting their horns, we notice that just as the eland metamorphosed to a unicorn in the first passage, so the horns that were sleeping eyes metamorphose into the headdresses of dowager operagoers in the second passage. In both passages, it is the process of metamorphosis itself, that is, transition and differentiation, that the contextualizing process seems to signify and sustain.

While this process of metamorphosis seems to depend on a fairly conventional interchange of literal and figurative value, closer inspection will reveal that the radical disjuncture between these levels of discourse actually discloses the threshold of a second-order reference, which then obviates the division between them. This is almost schematically illustrated in the catechismal progress of the doctor's monologue, each episode of which is solicited by a question from Nora or Felix demanding elucidation of their relations with Robin. In these instances, the interrogatory context denotes a set of previously established expectations. After all, a question demands an answer. Thus, it presupposes a determinate frame of reference. Because the doctor's inquisitors scrupulously observe the logical protocol of linear narrative, that protocol ironically binds them to a fatalistic fulfillment of their worst fears. For they ask questions that appeal to an absolute truth and seek in the answers a redemptive way back to the originary failure of their love. Their respect for the order of linear narrative delineates a literal perspective of meaning, but the doctor's replies do not fall within this literal (and determinate) perspective: they are its figural complement. An examination of the questions and the replies will show how we must revise our expectations about the sense that metaphor makes in this novel.

Indeed, the catechismal exchange between Felix and the doctor reveals how our changing expectations about metaphor implicate us in a rethinking of the stable narrative forms of fable and parable that are so tightly knit into the fabric of this text. Like Barnes's metaphors, the typically static tableau of fable and parable are here pressed into the service of a radically transitive, predicative intelligence.[14]

Felix asks, "Why did she [Robin] marry me?" (113), as if to fix a cause for the tragic effects of his life, to ritualize it and render it subject to a repeatable absolution. The doctor replies with a gesture that, in its resolute obliquity, points a path that only the reader of his fiction can follow since it crosses the frontier of the character's experiences. He says, "Take the case of the horse who knew too much" (113), and with this diversion he executes a catachrestic leap, radically revising the contextual priorities of the original question. Superficially, the doctor appears to propose that the horse is an analogue for Felix's own plight. Perhaps this is the only satisfactory answer to Felix's question, since, in his obsessive devotion to the past, his passion for belonging, he is a natural child of repetition. Furthermore, the logic of the doctor's retort accords with our expectation of how a metaphoric vehicle effectively dislodges a context of meaning from the perspective of familiarity that otherwise tarnishes its truthful gleam. But neither the elaboration of this vehicle nor Felix's inability to comprehend this turn of O'Connor's mind accords well with the expectation that metaphor should explicate a previous context of meaning and bridge contextual gaps by disclosing a covert similarity.

Instead, as in previous instances of metaphoric extension in *Nightwood*, the imagistic particulars of the metaphor seem to follow an unannounced semantic protocol rather than an explicit contextual rule: "She [the horse] was in mourning for something taken away from her in a bombardment in the war— by the way . . . she stood, that something lay between her hooves—she stirred no branch, though her hide was a river of sorrow." The passage culminates in a quick montage of similes, each of which further abstracts the contextual limits: "her eyelashes were gray and black, like the eyelashes of a nigger and at her buttocks' soft center a pulse throbbed like the fiddle" (113). Since these metaphors must appear incongruous at best and misleading at worst, the intelligibility of the montage depends upon understanding interruption (the motor of montage) as an organizational principle rather than simply an obstacle to sense; that is, the metaphor of the horse is a point of departure rather than a reservoir of accumulated meanings.

The telling moment of the passage in which this elaborate montage occurs is Felix's response. It is a perfect index of the distance between the character's and the reader's perspectives: "the baron, studying the menu said, 'The Petherbridge woman called on me'" (113). Felix's obliviousness to the doctor's lengthy digression is the measure of his comprehension and thus equally a measure of his incoherence. Ironically, "the horse who knew too much" may be taken as a token of the limits of character-centered narrative. For the knowledge generated (for the reader) by the doctor's metaphors is directly a product of the negation implicit in Felix's calculated obliviousness. It is intelligible only through Felix's characteristic noncomprehension. The answer to the question precludes the questioner. Typically, after every one of Nora's and Felix's entreaties to the oracle of the night, each is left speechless or willfully ignores the doctor's pronouncements, opening a chasm in the dialogical premise of the scene.

This negation of dialogue is virtually parodic, as it makes another implicit analogy between Felix and the horse. For the "something taken away" is present to the horse as an absence between her hooves and is futhermore a subtle hint of the horse's own disappearance behind the successive metaphoric screens of the river of sorrow, the nigger's eyelashes, the throbbing buttocks. The meaning of this passage, in light of Felix's impotence to engage its imagistic material and the consequent force of contextual displacements that structure it, is inextricable from the process of suspension and absence that I have alleged to be the structural crux of the narrative.

Generally speaking, literal meaning uses denotative value as a signified and figurative meaning uses denotative value as a signifier. As in the case of classical theories of metaphor, this understanding presupposes the exclusivity of both modes, granting priority to the former. But the relationship between the literal context reflected in Felix's question and the figurative context of the doctor's reply is such that the figurative meaning uses the literal as a signifier, raising the dynamic interaction between them to a level of significance that ordinarily would obtain only in the subordination of one to the other. The logical priorities dictated by the literal-figurative dichotomy are thus made conspicuously relative. As in the example of the lie, denotative value becomes a variable of usage, not an a priori determinant of experience. Ultimately, the doctor's response addresses Felix's question not by complying with the implicit point of the query, but rather by manipulating the question as a point of departure for his own narrative activity.

The linguistic coherence that this practice offers, in the midst of *Nightwood*'s incoherence, is boldly announced in another catachrestic exchange between Nora Flood and Dr. O'Connor. Possessed with the same helpless longing Felix expressed to the doctor in an attempt to mythify his own desire, Nora exclaims her inability to distinguish her desire for Robin from her desire for herself. "What shall I do?" she asks. The Doctor replies: "Make bird nests with your teeth" (28). From the logically precarious threshold of this retort, he relates the "case" of his English friend who had the birds queueing up at her windows, "holding onto their eggs as hard as they can like a man waiting at a toilet door for someone who had decided to read *The Decline and Fall of the Roman Empire*."

Like Felix, Nora registers the doctor's advice by ignoring it. Couched as it is in a familiar parable form of conventional narrative art, the doctor's digressive tale paradoxically subverts the narrative with the obtrusion of a competing *telos*. This new teleology is abruptly disjunctive with the relationships that otherwise establish Nora's continuity with the plot of the novel. For the attentive reader of *Nightwood*, however, it is precisely the disruptive pattern of metaphoric transitions dismembering the narrative that promises the richest exfoliations of this text—provided we treat disjuncture itself as the threshold of interpretation. For as we saw in the imagistic correspondence between the eland/unicorn and the beast cutting horns, where there is narrative discontinuity in *Nightwood*, there is often imagistic coherence to belie the impression of formless drift and suggest new criteria of relatedness.

So it is not surprising that in the paragraph immediately preceding Nora's question—What should I do?—we find that Barnes offers another cue for contextual cross-reference that seems to belie the immediate contextual chaos. In this paragraph, the doctor primes Nora's question with the metaphor of a horse, once again ostensibly a parable for the loss posited in Robin's person: "Once in war time I saw a dead horse that had been lying long against the ground. Time and the birds and its own last concentration had removed the body a great way from the head. As I looked upon that head my memory weighed for the lost body" (127).

The immediate effect of the retrospective cue taken here to contextualize the doctor's otherwise cryptic admonition, "Make bird nests with your teeth," is to suggest a connection between the birds of time and the birds that are holding their eggs against time's tumultuous flow. Clearly the causal logic imputed by this imagistic continuity is the same as that which governs conventional theories of trope and the literal-figurative dualism that orders already contextualized meaning. Hence we would expect that the birds in one passage determine the meaning of birds in another. While I do not dispute the causality that plays ominously between these passages, I hasten to point out that in this case the causal link is based only on imagistic content. The content is unifying because it motivates difference and variation, not because it fosters a repetition of like meanings. Indeed, if we assume for a moment the opposite point of view, the parable-metaphor of the horse who knew too much would, of course, appear to have prefigured the horse whose weight is memory, thereby extending the theme of loss from Felix to Nora. Yet while the birds in this metaphor provisionally embellish the theme of loss, their subsequent extension through another metaphoric transition unexpectedly implies the reversal of loss. Dependent on the mouth-forged nests of the doctor's "English friend," the queueing birds of time suggest domestication of the scavenging instinct with which the birds served the initial motive of metaphor: to represent the temporal flight that (as it is personified in the protean figure of Robin Vote) ruthlessly scavenges the lives of Barnes's other characters.

It is time, after all, that the desiring subject is keenly aware he or she will never survive. And thus we are forcefully reminded that it is the doctor's own "mouth-forged" metaphors that, by their disruption of scenic logic, are intended to anesthetize the pain of time's passage for his audience. With a characteristic sense of paradox, the doctor defends his dissembling "wont" in a moment of undisguised lucidity: "Do you know what has made me the greatest liar this side of the moon? Telling my stories to people like you to take the mortal agony out of their guts" (135). We can now see that the doctor's metaphorizing therapy curiously obeys the admonition he brought to Nora— make bird nests with your teeth—by redeeming the significance of single acts or images to a freer multiplicity of perspective. In his willful proliferation of disparate images, he vies with the proliferating moments of time. In its ungraspable multiplicity, this proliferation inevitably escapes the resolute singlemindedness of every well-formed desire. Nora's fate, and implicitly the fate of her fellows, is sealed precisely insofar as all three characters seal themselves off from the genius of this multiplicity. Paradoxically, however, the stoic oblivion that insulates them from the doctor's rhetoric is the vehicle of the reader's imaginative mobility within the text.

III

The doctor commences his monologue with the admonition: "I have a narrative but you will be hard pressed to find it." In light of the compositional strategies already discussed here, we may take this as the undisguised challenge of a prose artist whose entire *oeuvre* emphatically reminds us that narrative is a practice as well as a product of verbal representation. In a pronouncement that bears the full conceptual burden of Djuna Barnes's notoriously "difficult" prose, Dr. O'Connor goes on to decry the impotence of a language that merely gives a word for a thing and not its "alchemy" (83). The "alchemy of the word" (and it is the metaphor of alchemy that suggests that the word is finally indistinguishable from the thing) vividly conjures the quality of Barnes's prose that transcends orthodox strategies of figuration, those which only make the unfamiliar express the familiar. In contrast to the hierarchy of literal and figural values privileged by I. A. Richards's notion of the metaphoric "vehicle," the fluidity of literal and figural contexts in *Nightwood* renders the contextually inert image a productive perspective. The significance of the image is in the new connections it fosters and not in its transcendence to an already contextualized meaning. In this way, the status of the image in *Nightwood* is qualified as radically as the structure of character. The historical pretext of the image, to present an autonomous expression, is betrayed to the contingency of contextual metamorphoses. Here, the image expresses the need to assimilate that contingency.

Felix Volkbein apprehends the danger of this contingency and takes refuge in the fixed image as a bulwark against change. This is especially apparent when he confesses that Robin appeals to him chiefly as the iconography of unmediated devotion: "An image is a stop the mind makes between uncertainties" (111). In fact the most elaborate metaphors in *Nightwood* are images that would remain static (in Felix's sense) by their evocation of an already contextualized meaning, except that the implied transcendence of immediate contextual particulars in Barnes's prose always entails a reorganization of logical priorities. Nevertheless, the catachrestic trope disrupting narrative continuity in *Nightwood* does not, like so much of the playful rhetoric of contemporary metafiction and antifiction, find its fulfillment in ironic confession of its own artificiality. In *Nightwood*, ironic recognitions of the text's facticity are meaningfully integrated only as they make new points of departure the burden of their expression.

In his mock-Nietzschean "will to lie," Dr. O'Connor concurs that the legitimacy of every statement is a function of its ability to invoke a new context. Almost as though Barnes's protagonist shares an awareness of the narcissistic traps that fiction writers unwittingly lay for themselves, the doctor observes that the "chiefest danger of all" is the person who presents herself as a static image. This person (Robin Vote) presents herself as a picture "forever arranged." Such an image, such a person, poses itself as an ideality: epistemologically self-sufficient and thus portending a metaphysical "truth." Concerning the theme of love and desire in *Nightwood*, we may say that the static image is the prick of desire that nonetheless does not yield to the processes of the desiring self.

The destabilized metaphor operates precisely by submitting the image to a process of transition and transformation that augments its discursive power without hypostatizing its discursive value. This "renegade trope" makes the image a vehicle for transformation. Thus, in the fiction of Djuna Barnes, metaphor supplants dramatic action as the formal arbiter of contextual differences that make narrative movement originally possible. I have already noted that the desires of her characters are both parodied and superseded in the production of the text of *Nightwood* itself. This argument is most persuasive in the rhetorical coincidence of character and author in *Nightwood* and in its characteristic extension of metaphors to subvert the hegemony of literal meaning. Again, I associate literal meaning with plot insofar as plot denotes a univocal contextual purpose.

Barnes's desire to nullify discriminations between the internal (dramatic) and external (authorial) levels in this novel is nowhere more explicit than in the culminating episode of her narrative. For the last chapter of *Nightwood*, "The Possessed," resolves itself in a portentous tableau, a static image, an icon of narrativity, precisely that "danger" with which Dr. O'Connor's monologue is so tragically obsessed. In "The Possessed," Robin Vote, described as utterly divested of her "motive power," and having come unconsciously to the threshold of Nora Flood's family chapel in America, encounters her nemesis in Nora's lunging guard dog. On an "altar" contrived of a candlelit madonna and a veritable bier of flowers, the two "go down" before each other, eye to eye in a passion of unrestrained animality:

> The dog began to cry then, running with her [Robin], head-on with her head, as if slowly and surely to circumvent her; soft and slow his feet went padding. He ran this way and that, low down in his throat crying, and she grinning and crying with him; crying in shorter and shorter spaces, moving head to head until she gave up, lying out, her hands beside her, her face turned and weeping; and the dog too gave up then, and lay down, his eyes bloodshot, his head flat along her knees. (170)

In the four "climactic" pages of this chapter, the familiar metaphorical displacements of Barnes's prose style are conspic-

uously absent. Simultaneously, the chapter marks the eclipse of
Dr. O'Connor and the resumption of the omniscient narrative
voice. For these reasons, the chapter seems to suggest continuity with a causally ordered sequence of events—that is to say,
with an orthodox narrative technique based on a succession of
episodes related to one another by a systematically diminishing
set of expectations. We must remember, however, that it is precisely such lucid causality—that is, the progressive reduction
of contextual discrepancies—that the precipitous rhetoric of
Djuna Barnes's narrative has preempted throughout the preceding 166 pages. The sudden apparent reversion to a literal
narrative in the final chapter is furthermore belied by the metaphoric resonance of its imagery, teasing a fairly conventional
metaphoric knowledge in its evocation of already contextualized figures; the literal "meet" of dog and woman here assumes
a fuller articulation of the metaphor of the "beast turning human" and unexpectedly realizes the doctor's earlier prophetic
pronouncement upon the fate binding Nora and Robin: "Nora
will leave that girl someday; but though these two are buried at
opposite ends of the earth one dog will find them both" (106).

Even with this return to an earlier image, the final chapter of
Nightwood does not occasion the climactic development of a latent image pattern. Rather, and more crucially, it incurs self-
consciousness about the relational hierarchy that conditions the
significance of such patterns in the first place. In effect, the
metaphoric dog (beast), which has been lurking within the doctor's monologue as a second-order meaning, leaps dramatically
into the foreground of this narrative to rout those meanings
constraining metaphor to a purely heuristic role. What was figurative in previous contexts becomes literal, thus inhibiting a
reader's attempt to value one over the other. Here is the repudiation of narrative levels that, I have argued, is the object
of the catachrestic metaphor in *Nightwood*. The blend of literal
and figural values coagulating *Nightwood*'s plot in the ultimate
tableau of "The Possessed" actually recapitulates the desires of
Barnes's characters. The representational prextext becomes a

context for compositional revisions and transformations that subsist only upon the freedom of new articulations. In much the same way that Dr. O'Connor usurps the idiom of the omniscient voice, here the omniscient narrator, usurping the doctor's metaphor, draws the reader in as witness to its duplicity.

Of course the lie, the duplicity of desire in *Nightwood*, breaches no idealism of truth. If language succeeds in effecting an openness to new experiences, it must proceed by differentiating the terms of its own expressiveness. In the doctor's own words, "the foetus of symmetry nourishes itself on cross purposes" (97). In its stylistic disjuncture from the rest of the novel, the apparent cross purposes of "The Possessed" have such force at the end of *Nightwood* because the chapter offers an analogue/repetition of the discontinuities that rend the preceding narrative, both thematically and stylistically. And because the last chapter must be read in light of all that comes before, it includes the insight that the novelistic text is always its own problem, over and above the problematic displayed by the conventions of character, plot, etc. Like catachrestic metaphor, the shaping device of Barnes's narrative, the imagistic stasis and contextual unanimity of this final chapter announce both a suspension of previous contextual norms and, therefore, a projection of new contextual predicates.

Because the projection of new contextual meanings in "The Possessed" functions as an analogue for the continual sliding of the literal sign under the figurative sign throughout *Nightwood*, it articulates an authorial reflexivity that complements the production of the text itself. "The Possessed" reminds us that, as readers, we are in the presence of a self-examining imagination, alive through the transformational character of Barnes's prose.

Having attempted to grasp the formal totality of *Nightwood*, we may return to the question that opened this chapter and thereby judge what Djuna Barnes has contributed to the idea of fiction. It is now possible to see how the play of desires mimed in the style of *Nightwood* returns us to one of the controlling interests of this work: contemplation of the problems of authorship. After all, it is not an uncommon suspicion among genre critics that the novel form arose to combat the anxiety of authorial self-consciousness —hence, the realist tradition that presents an ideological stance in the guise of representational fidelity to the real.

In the attempt to skate safely over the disruptive surface of Barnes's prose, literary critics ironically defer to the very content that its style makes problematic. The touchstone of most such readings of this novel is the milieu of Jacobean doom, which they argue is evoked in its intrigue-woven plot, the emotional torment of its fate-crossed lovers, and its dramatic dissemination through the tropes of sexual desire. Most important, however, the allusion to Jacobean tragedy offers critics a convenient historical precedent for the troublesome convolutions of Barnes's prose. Critics, citing the rhetorical density of Jacobean verse drama, invariably find occasion for reducing the stylistic motivations of *Nightwood* to the lurid psychology of the Jacobean ethos.[15] Ruled by the curse of irredeemable sin and obsessive remorse, the world of Jacobean theater is indeed strikingly close to the solipsistic darkness of Barnes's characters. And insofar as *Nightwood* chronicles the self-destruction of Nora, Jenny, and Felix, it likewise constitutes a familiar "story" of the limits of human love. But the sentimental banalities to which such a "story" always threatens to reduce itself have the concomitant effect of trivializing the rhetorical complications that drew attention to the story in the first place.

I have already suggested, however, that the formalist alternatives to this weak thematization can err in the same tendency toward abstraction. This is true whether the application of formalist method implies simply a systematic collation of structural features or the extrapolation of an analytical principle like Joseph Frank's spatial form. Whether the meaning of *Nightwood* inheres, as Frank says, in the atemporal simultaneity of imagery (that is, the mosaic versus narrative construction of meaning) or in what a more recent commentator has called a "non-representational," Valéryean orchestration of musical effects, the result of such claims is to turn the text toward an ideality comparable with that "chiefest danger" posed to author and character alike: fixed image.[16]

As we have seen, the principal danger inherent in the fixed image is its illusion of metaphysical depth: that remote truth to which the "lie" of ordinary human experience stands in perpetual debt. A complementary danger of formalist criticism of *Nightwood* designates the novel a work of "poetic prose." "Poetry" is invoked as an irreducible quality of style and so, inadvertently, as a transcendent value of the text. Spatial form, for example, aptly describes the perceptual constraints upon reading *Nightwood* but censors any particular meanings that do not merely recapitulate its formal limits. In fact, for all his excited heralding of a "new novel" in *Nightwood*, Joseph Frank's explications ultimately recoil upon the familiar themes of love, loneliness, and tragic desire—without acknowledging how these themes are dispersed along new conceptual axes, and how by virtue of these disjunctures they transcend the fictive world projected through unities of character, plot, setting. The category of "poetic prose" remains abstract from the effects of *Nightwood*'s narrative because it perversely designates poetry as a metaphor for the intricate working of Barnes's prose style, rather than elucidating a specific function of language that, like the metaphoricity of Barnes's own prose, would dispose our familiar relations of representation to a new organization of reality.

To speak of form in terms of linguistic function rather than apostrophized structures would, of course, entail a precise account of how Barnes's technique emerges from the limits of conventional narrative and therefore how the characters, plot, etc. yield an explanation of the novel's highly original form. For this reason, I have argued that the question of how the text produces an image of its productivity must offer the most reliable account of what it means. Likewise, the threshold of authorial self-consciousness supplies the greatest critical leverage for a full appreciation of Barnes's accomplishment, since that self-consciousness fully dramatizes the productive agency of the text as a presupposition of its dramatic projections.

In the throes of his idolatrous love for Robin Vote, Felix Volkbein embodies the risks inherent for character and reader alike in any judgment of meaning that does not include the complete mediations of *its own desire* for meaning. In his obsession with a past that exists only in the improvisational frenzy of the present moment, Felix bows down to the mirage of a metaphysical truth presented by the image of the beloved. Ordinary metaphor bears much the same resemblance to literal meaning as Felix's desires for another person bear to that person. In addition, the structure of ordinary metaphor undergoes the same subversion as Felix's desires, where the catachrestic extremity of Barnes's prose forces the integration of literal and figurative values along a single axis of displacement and articulation. In *Nightwood*, the desire of one character for another, whose very otherness implies a prior and ideally formed meaning, is consonant with Barnes's subversion of metaphoric structures that appear to be only a re-presentation of already formulated knowledge. We have seen how the idealism of love is undone in Felix's and Nora's realization that the desiring self only augments its own processes. Therefore, we may now assert that the analogous structure of authorial desire *to represent* will find its most profound fulfillment in the self-production of the text. Otherwise the author risks falling into the ironic despair of Barnes's characters. The desire to make fictions, like the desire for another person, takes on significance when it becomes a way of diversifying the structure of the self rather than capturing a specular other.

Therefore, when we ask how *Nightwood* may be understood as a novel—recognizing its obvious conventional deficiencies—we participate in a significant reformulation of genre expectations. I believe the motive for this reformulation is authorized by the very critique of novelistic assumptions that *Nightwood* performs upon itself: a tropological obtrusiveness that sets character, plot, and setting quite visibly within the creative faculty of authorship. I have said that the self-contestations characteristic of Djuna Barnes's fiction are perhaps focused more dramatically in the rhetorical stillness of the final chapter. This chapter denies the pretext of esthetic unity signaled by its finality. In this denial it epitomizes the disjunctive rhetoric that organizes the rest of the novel. Barnes thus invites the perceptive reader to see that the insufficiency of "The Possessed" as a self-sustaining narrative gesture, that is, a literary coda (the coda is logically assimilable to the structure of ordinary metaphor by its formally distinct but conceptually encompassing pattern of meaning), reaffirms the supplementary function that has generated the text to this point.

This point is clearest at the juncture of the last two chapters of *Nightwood*. At the conclusion of the penultimate chapter, the doctor's apocalyptic benediction for Nora, Jenny, and Felix— "now nothing but wrath and weeping"—makes his narrative appear to be anything but "hard to find," as he warned at the start of his monologue. For the despair he gives utterance to here clearly enunciates the teleological order by its repetition and culmination of the tragic impasse to which all of Barnes's characters have arrived. Following upon this moment, however, the anticlimactic "supplementation" of "The Possessed," with its repetition of the gesture of narrative ending, reveals an otherwise disguised contingency of authorial presence ordinarily repressed through the powerful sublimations of plot *dénouement* and *catharsis*. Perhaps this ending suggests that the true "tragedy" of *Nightwood* lies not in the characters's failures but in the reader's failure to acknowledge the reconstructive possibilities latent in authorial self-consciousness: in the failure of the reader to see how the stories of the characters must inevitably fold back into the processes of story telling, the function of which is, after all (as the doctor's performance so eloquently attests), to renew experience.

In the next chapter we shall see how the act of renewing experience through the structures of metaphor is implicitly a contestation of the large, impersonal, deterministic forces of ideology. The narrative artist who works with metaphor conceives his or her work as a meticulous extrication from the snares of a "self-authenticating" language that paradoxically can speak only the various dissimulations of history.

4
THE
PARODY
OF
FATE

SECOND SKIN
AND THE DEATH OF
THE NOVEL

> Recently I did formulate a kind of theory of fiction
> which can be expressed in a few words. It seems to me
> that fiction should achieve revenge for all the indignities
> of our childhood; it should be an act of rebellion against
> all the constraints of the conventional pedestrian
> mentality around us. Surely it should destroy
> conventional morality. I suppose all this is to say that to
> me the act of writing is criminal. If the act of the
> revolutionary is one of supreme idealism, it's also
> criminal. Obviously I think that the so-called criminal
> act is essential to our survival.
>
> John Hawkes,
> in "A Conversation on *The Blood Oranges*
> between John Hawkes and Robert Scholes"

Practicing novelists often put forth theories of fiction espousing
the creed of a mighty renunciation. In its most banal version,
this renunciation reduces to the old standoff of esthetic versus
normative values: the esthete's disavowal of quotidian reality.
But let us suppose that renunciation entails a more scrupulous
awareness of the presuppositions of authorship vis-à-vis the authority of an already constructed world. Then it may bear eloquent witness to the complicity of esthetic values with the ideological milieu that spawns them. In this chapter we shall see

how John Hawkes's "criminal" negation actually entails an appropriation of the symbolic order he seeks to escape. Thus Hawkes's esthetic credo may teach us something about the relation of narrative desire to the forms of desire we inhabit as living ideology.

Like Djuna Barnes, Hawkes's originality in this regard stems from his use of the trope of metaphor. Any satisfying critical account of Hawkes's prose style must begin here. Indeed it is particularly apt that a stylist who works so emphatically with metaphor should lead us to contemplate the relation between ideology and art, since metaphor is the "criminal" disruption par excellence of ideological discourse. Metaphor works within habits of linguistic usage to estrange them from familiar intentions. Hawkes's metaphor in particular forces the habitual to disclose new meaning by giving free play to otherwise repressed discursive contingencies. If we are going to accept Hawkes's esthetic credo, we will understand that ideology also must be forced to disclose its own contradictions within the terms of the artist's esthetic renunciation. As his novels make clear, only by this means do the novelists of renunciation make of their inescapable situatedness a new situation.

What critics usually identify as Hawkes's break with tradition is paradoxically continuous with the intellectual concerns of other great narrative artists who found their own "radical" terms within other traditions. In Flaubert's famous letter about *Madame Bovary*, for example, the pressure of ideology is acknowledged as an impossibly rigorous defense of style:

> What I should like to write is a book about nothing . . . without any external support which would be held together by the inner strength of its style . . . a book that would have almost no subject or at least in which the subject would be almost invisible. . . . Form as it becomes more skillful is attenuated; it abandons all liturgy, all rules, all measures; it deserts the epic for the novel . . . it no longer

recognizes any orthodoxy and is as free as the individual will that produces it.[1]

For the Flaubertian novelist, significant form lies in a renunciation of despotic orthodoxies. But rather than merely proliferating the automatic ironies spawned in negation, Flaubert's stance asserts the productive potential of negation. Negation confirms the mark of "individual will" within any production it may entail. Joseph Conrad, discovering himself besieged within a stifling circle of "fellows, gods, passions," legitimates the independent authority of authorship in terms of a negation that loudly echoes Flaubert's esthetic of detachment. Conrad writes that for every imaginative effort finding its inspiration in the reality of form and sensation, "all adventure, all love, every success is resumed in the supreme energy of an act of renunciation. It is the uttermost limit of our powers."[2]

Both Flaubert and Conrad seem to be natural fathers for Hawkes's criminal persona: their fictions situate the reader well within that region of human imagination that demands suspension of worldly appearance in order to free its own articulation. For both authors, a self-referencing style is the double articulation upon which productive negation depends. The pulp dreams of Emma Bovary, which disrupt the worldly order of her marriage, are in turn troped by the relativity of Flaubert's own prose strategies. Emma's daydreaming vitiates the hierarchy of conventional narrative levels (literal and figurative, real and imaginary) an order that usually fixes expectations along the lines of accepted social relations. In the famous agricultural fair scene of *Madame Bovary*, Flaubert, insisting that "everything sound simultaneously," collapses the three social classes depicted there into a seamless tableau, subsuming the hierarchical levels of protagonist-antagonist, primary-secondary actions all within an encompassing textual code. Similarly, in the ever-receding narrative horizon of Conrad's *Lord Jim*, the specter of Jim's "veiled opportunity" tropes the successive veils of narrative authority, veils that only disclose the process of their own unveiling. Thus Conrad exposes the machinery of narrative in order to dispel the illusion of spontaneous life—how we ordinarily naturalize the process of reading novels.

Yet one insurmountable obstacle remains in understanding epistemological renunciations such as these. For Flaubert, Conrad, and Hawkes, the wish to "destroy the constraints of pedestrian mentality" is always intractably bound within, and so doubly resistant to, a use of language forever reminded of its own a posteriori status: its own literariness. Since language is always already "there" for these writers, it can be ironically most articulate for them only as a self-admittedly inadequate gesture to reify the "individual will"; they insist only upon the reflexive freedom to express that desire.

Of course, the theoretical novelist's desire to articulate the ground instead of the content of the genre's expressive possibilities is incompatible with the conventional modes of authorial presence in literature. Authorial presence is commonly revealed in the ironic distance between character and narration, even though this conventionalized distance begs the question of the self-conscious authority of the novelist, where the writers I am discussing stake their esthetic claims. As Georg Lukács contends in *The Theory of the Novel*, a hero's progress toward some ultimate knowledge is always tragic in the context of the creative activity of the novelist.[3] Typically, heroes cannot match the set of authorial predicates that projected their worlds. Consequently, the world betrays the hero's contingency, the partiality of the hero's view. This partiality is dramatized within what Roland Barthes has called the "reality effect,"[4] the fixing of signifying relations within which character is recognizable as an ever-wavering contingency of plot. For critics like Lukács, representational fidelity lies in the ultimate reconciliation of character and world: the joining of character and plot predicates in a totalizing complementarity. This complementarity is the domain of literal meaning. Literal meaning also relies upon contextual homogeneity for its intelligibility and so depends implicitly on the devices of narrative closure to complete its sense. This literal closure is precisely the ideological situation to which the writers I have mentioned refuse to submit, and so I look to the figural level of discourse for a concept of narrative form more compatible with their claims.

I

The renunciatory stance of stylists like Flaubert, Conrad, and Hawkes may be linked with the inherent discontinuity of metaphor: by disrupting the signifier-signified relation, metaphor poses the possibility of destroying contextual homogeneity and the standards of representational authenticity that are founded upon them. Metaphor still obeys the integrative mandate of creative act. But in the works of experimental writers who exploit the disruptive tension of metaphor, the integrative function is rendered intelligible within a radically revised perspective. As we have seen in the case of Djuna Barnes, for many "experimental" writers, metaphor does not concede identity with a prior recognizable ground of meaning. Such writers do not accept that metaphor must involve the representation of familiar relations in a new guise. Rather, for them metaphor creates a new contextual rule precisely in the consistency of its displacements as they are sustained across disparate contextual barriers.

I have chosen John Hawkes's novel *Second Skin*[5] to explore further the potential innovations for fictive form that are latent in the structure of metaphor. The transformational flux evoked by the reptilian metaphor of Hawkes's title connotes the sliding of contextual markers that produce metaphoric meaning. Furthermore, *Second Skin* permits us to explore the syntactical basis of metaphoric extravagance. In the novel, the contextual displacements of metaphor are compounded by the cumulative syntax of Hawkes's prose to a virtually catachrestic extremity. Hawkes permutes metaphoric imagery over extended patterns of syntactical dependency. This has the effect of dispersing the predicates that established the metaphor in the first place. This exaggerated syntactical contingency consequently seems to subvert the rationalizing and recuperative aim of the figurative gambit. Extravagant extensions of metaphors—over three or four image groups—create a confusion in contextual priorities.

Second Skin is narrated in the first person by an ex-naval officer, junior grade. He mockingly calls himself "Skipper" as if to anticipate the interrogation of conventional narrative authority that this novel takes up through its rhetorical complications. The moment Skipper attempts to relate his personal history, he falls into the practice of figurative and syntactical suspension:

> Say . . . that it [the narrative] is the chronicle of recovery, the history of courage, the dead reckoning of my romance, the act of memory, the dance of shadows. (162)

The paradox of this brief invocation is its anaphoric gesture toward repetition, the appositional pretext of renaming, which quite uncharacteristically displays a radically differentiated set of assumptions for the appositional phrases as each inaugurates a new contextual pattern. Of course, the sense of this passage is not especially problematic if we psychologize the rhetorical effects in terms of the conventions of first-person narration. But the underlying assumptions are not ultimately reconcilable with the assumptions of first-person narration. The structure of character is in fact antithetical to the operation of Hawkes's prose and the epistemological stance of his fiction, because character is usually construed retrospectively out of a closed set of predicates. The burden of such a structure is to give credible cause to the effects of character development, to reconcile the synecdochic dispersal of character traits with a transcendent principle of identity.

The interdependency of syntax and trope evident in Skipper's litany of historical epithets, however, belies the predicative closure typically effected by the "unities" of character.[6] Hawkes's metaphoricity, like his appositional attenuations of narrative predicates, works through a strategy of interruptions. Hawkes disdains the symmetry of literal and figural values that harnesses the tamer metaphors of conventional fiction to the expository burdens of a linear narrative. Hawkes's prose is therefore not compatible with Lukács's model of ironic plot structure certifying the "facts" of fiction through the privileging of a literal meaning. Lukács's model text dramatizes its internal contingencies (in their partiality) merely as they reflect a more inclusive predication: not as they revise the predicative authority implemented through that inclusiveness.[7]

Second Skin begins at a proverbial narrative beginning. As it is for God the creator, so it is for Skipper: the problem of creating is the problem of naming. Because Skipper self-consciously bills his story as "history," the problem of naming raises the issue of truth in much the same way that it is raised by the tenets of realist fiction; it is the adequacy of the text to an a priori condition. The possessive pun in "history" clearly confuses the notion of objective causality—the propriety of the name—with self-authorizing cause. This confusion is, of course, the ground contested by fact and fiction. Appropriately, from the very first chapter of this narrative, "Naming Names," Skipper's narcissistic invocation of the muse raises the question of the adequacy of the text to the world—but without the clear enunciation of a correspondent determinate rule. This forces our recognition of the conditionality of Skipper's narrative practice:

> I will tell you in a few words who I am: lover of the hummingbird that darts to the flower beyond the rotted sill where my feet are propped: lover of bright needlepoint and the bright stitching finger of humorless old ladies bent to their sweet and infamous designs: lover of parasols made from the same puffy stuff as a young girl's underwear: still lover of that small naval boat which somehow survived the distressing years of my life between her decks. But most of all, lover of my harmless sanguine self. (1)

Like the opening gesture of every narrative, metaphor is also a practice of nomination. I have shown that metaphor is conventionally founded on a prior rule or resemblance, authorizing the transfer of the proper name to a new object. In this opening passage of *Second Skin*, Skipper cites his epithetical guises of love as apparent metaphors for self—but with imagistic detail that thwarts any easy resemblance. Strictly speaking, these epithets are not proper metaphors. But the anaphoric syntax of this passage evokes a metaphoric tension among the separate images. This tension nonetheless remains stubbornly unresolvable. Even as a juxtaposition of autonomous images, the hummingbird, the old ladies, the parasols, and the naval boat do not appear to confirm the narrator's identity as "most of all lover of my harmless and sanguine self." Indeed, these images are important less because of their content than as an index of how Skipper makes connections.

Because the images are elaborated to entire descriptive vignettes, the kernel images of this passage make semantic and thematic intelligibility even more inaccessible. Instead of reducing differences and confirming character as the pretext for juxtaposition, this passage—proliferating differences—calls the motive of the juxtaposition itself into question. The fact of syntactical juxtaposition alone might suffice in some novels for a successful resolution of contextual unity. But syntactical construal by itself cannot grasp the term of resemblance that should bind all of the epithets to a common ground of representation. It can only take that term for granted. In this way, the fact of syntactical juxtaposition could be construed nominally as a record of the narrator's personal chronology apart from any linguistic characterization or representation of character. But such an interpretation, ignoring the rhetorical forms of its dissemination (and in this, its complicity with a larger structure of discourse), only turns the prose of the first-person narrator into a cryptic metaphor for itself, instead of providing a way to explore its epistemological status. Therefore, it is necessary to find some other means of weighing the unifying inference of

Hawkes's strategy of juxtapositions against the dispersive particularity that articulates them.

Because *Second Skin* is presented as a self-contesting narrative—everywhere jeopardizing its own continuity—it is particularly unhelpful to consider Skipper's persona independent of the rhetorical devices by which he presents himself. Such an explanation fails to account for the verbal agency needed to free the text from the ideological restraints of narrative convention with which it so demonstrably struggles. Rather, let me say that the apparent predicative indeterminacy of Skipper's opening benediction in "Naming Names," instead of posing an obstacle to sense, is the operative condition of the narrative development it unfolds. Furthermore, this indeterminacy must be assimilated as a condition of interpreting the text.

As I have shown, this principle of predicative suspense is instrumental from the beginning of Hawkes's novel. Skipper's nominations in the first chapter self-consciously attempt to presage the ultimate fate of his characters. Ironically, Skipper's litany of character names, echoing the conventional novelist's ordination of a "living world," ordains instead a genealogy of suicides: his father, his mother, his wife Gertrude, and his daughter Cassandra. The irony is compounded in the actual names; intended to evoke the identity and fate of real historical beings, they betray the most outrageous literary derivations. Their allegorical resonances invoke the theme of fate as an artifact of past reading and so undermine the self-authorizing closure presupposed by the fact of fictive naming.

Contrary to what might be expected, the reader's effort to invoke Skipper's past as the genetic code of this fiction, to locate a determinate origin, inevitably subverts the very authority upon which such reading habits are originally predicated. For while the past-tense retrospective cast of the first chapter appropriately subordinates the past-tense episodes of the second and third chapters to a compelling linear logic, the fourth chapter resumes in a present tense strangely inconsistent with the preceding chapters. The legacy of death that seemed to give Skipper retrospective authority in chapter one seems to have been transmuted to the generative authority of the "artificial inseminator" in chapter four by the mere announcement of Catalina Kate's pregnancy. A narrative that appeared to be based on the recovery of the past is now made contingent on a future outcome. This transformation is perhaps the best metaphor of all for the process of reading Hawkes's fiction. The illusion of attaining knowledge is shed in the slippage between contextual predicates and the relation of closure that they seem to posit. Like the chronological markers of linear narrative (that is, the signifiers of narrative fate) in this fiction, the fixed coordinates of plot, character, and setting are subverted and become signifiers for the very process that sustains their self-contesting expressiveness and yields the imaginary richness of the work.

The complementary syntactical and semantic suspension organizing the language of John Hawkes's fiction may now be generally explicated as a strategy for confronting the limits of novelistic convention. Despite his famous disavowal of plot, character, theme, and setting, Hawkes has frequently said that in *Second Skin* he became interested in parodying the conventions of the novel. Indeed, Hawkes's choice of first person—bound as it is to the devices of linear narrative—seems to reveal a willingness to acknowledge that even the most experimental esthetic is complicit in conventions. At the same time, he claims the freedom that only acknowledgment of this complicity can endow. Hawkes seems to be aware that the first-person narrator, unable to disguise his or her origin within the self-representing reflex of narrative will, is automatically trapped by the myth of a naive *mimesis*.

The record of this paradoxical awareness among novelists goes at least as far back as Tristram Shandy's first-person attempt to conceive a narrative in true proportion to the dimensions of real space and time. Especially in those chapters that strain to capture the moment of his own conception (the only possible authoritative beginning), Tristram illustrates that fidelity to life demands a multiplicity unmatched by those conventions of narrative art suggesting the pretext of faithfulness to reality in the first place.[8] Perhaps Hawkes's thirst for "revenge" upon childhood indignities really addresses the epistemological naiveté to which the narrative artist is betrayed by the conventional rhetorical postures of the genre. In those conventions he or she is caught unwittingly in a contradiction. The narrative artist stands between the representational authority looming in the formal devices of narrative and the concomitant awareness that implementation of such devices only denotes the choice they embody, that is, evidence of the author's own facticity.

II

The unabashed facticity of Skipper's narrative keeps the imagination of this narrative alive amidst omnipresent death. Death is the closure that looms in the past-tense voice adopted by Skipper at the beginning of his fiction. Excavating the discursive ground that Hawkes so widely travels in this fiction, Roland Barthes says the preterite tense serves as the "cornerstone" of narrative because it "presupposes a world which is constructed, elaborated, self-sufficient, reduced to significant lines."[9] Perhaps Hawkes's most acutely parodic device is aimed at this pretext, embodied for his purposes in the character of Skipper's daughter, Cassandra. In one sense Skipper's narrative is the story of his attempt to keep his daughter from succumbing to the family fate. It is after all the fate of all tragic characters to die in obedience to some transcendent, totalizing principle, and there is a distinct element of parody in the overt archetypicality of Hawkes's plot insofar as it tempts such expectations. Cassandra's suicidal inertia does supply the narrative thrust of the book's linear plot. But perhaps we can see an even more elaborate parodic design behind this characterization (and the threat of closure that it portends) when we realize that Hawkes invokes a conspicuous complement and antidote to Cassandra's fixed fate, that is, the disjunctive present and future-tense episodes of Catalina Kate's "floating island." While Skipper cannot prevent Cassandra's death in the fatalistic time of the linear plot, he is able in the counterlinear plot of Kate's island to mitigate the inexorability of Cassandra's death. When it can finally be told, her death is deliberately troped by the birth of Kate's child. While Skipper's role seems to be defined by his efforts to avoid the closure of Cassandra's suicide, the stylistic and chronological disjunctures that disclose that plot belie—by their illumination of reconstructive possibilities—the inevitability of that closure. Thus, authorial power is revealed through its successful troping of characterological fate.

This apparent conflict between character and author is intimated thematically in the "originary" trauma of Skipper's youth. Ostensibly, this narrative moment offers causation for the linear plot of the novel:

> my father had begun my knowledge of death as a lurid truth . . . but my mother had extended it towards the promise of mystery. (8)

Early in the novel, the twin deaths of Skipper's parents are presented as a deliberate schematization of reality. Skipper, the sole witness to his father's suicide, is forced to confront this death as a brutal fact. His necessary passivity, fixing him with a burden of guilt as helplessly as any character in a novel, dooms him to a fatalistic reality. His mother, though, absenting him from the scene of her own death, permits him the liberty of imagining it and proffers the role of authorial atonement. Criticism of *Second Skin* has nurtured the conspicuously planted seed of this dichotomy between truth and mystery, reality and imagination (it is the final rhetorical flourish of the "Naming Names" chapter) into an imposing framing device within which one can enclose the otherwise wayward contradictions of the texts.[10] Under the influence of this structural imperative, critics say that the novel proposes an exchange of the fatalistic values of reality (character) for the redemptive values of imagination (author)—one metaphorically substituting for the other. This equation is specifically assimilable to the form of conventional trope. In our presupposition of a literal-figurative dichotomy, we traditionally legitimate the second term insofar as it serves as a token for the first, not as it assumes value in its own right. The fact is that Skipper's own understanding of narrative is based on his ability to organize reality as the interchange between poles of experience. Encountering evil everywhere, Skipper secures his own innocence in the guise of the victim.

Indeed, it is tempting to try to resolve the rhetorical duplicities of this fiction by a single unifying schema. But the disjunctive temporality of Skipper's narrative, along with his seeming inability to sustain a declarative statement that does not open syntactically upon a multiplicity of fresh possibilities, does not make this text conducive to a binary analysis whereby each meaning only reflects its dialectical partner. For this reason, we may assume that the stylistic imperatives of the novel imply a more deeply troubled predicament than the traumas of childhood could account for. Those traumas only elucidate the structure of character as a recuperative or substitutive trope rather than a constitutive trope which discloses the contingencies that are constructed within it. In order to understand how this fiction transcends character-centered structures of intelligibility, we must look for the devices of an extraneous authorial freedom.

While I have said provisionally that the polarity of reality and imagination appears to hold in tension the otherwise vagrant movements of Hawkes's rhetoric, this controlling opposition (reflected in Skipper's own desire to see himself as the perennial sacrificial victim of a death-dealing world) is precisely what is called into question by Skipper's reconstruction of the facts of his naked history. From the first pages of this novel, Skipper chooses to describe himself as a "large and innocent Iphigenia, betrayed on the beach," a ritual sacrifice to the shadowy knife blade of human evil. Conspicuously at the sacrificial heart of Skipper's experience aboard the USS *Starfish*—the episode that is the rhetorical center of this narrative—is Tremlow, the mutinous sailor. Pitting himself against Skipper's yielding innocence, Tremlow offers to reify the dichotomous ethos of victim and victimizer, good and evil, and to confirm the meaning of Skipper's life in a closed structure of signification. Posing as one of the avatars of evil, the perpetrator of a physical rape, Tremlow establishes Skipper's innocence as the functional complement of his own villainy. But by virtue of this mode of self-realization, Skipper would be reduced to the scribe of a prior text: mortality itself.

Skipper's every utterance would establish a relationship with a single set of conditions, the univocality of those conditions imposing a burden of truth that would be epistemologically insupportable. The insupportability of the single truth is evident in all of Skipper's efforts to rationalize his survival as the fate of the victim. Every attempt to control the threat of destruction by putting it under the sign of the good-evil dichotomy breeds internal contradictions that interpose the very distance between Skipper's language and events that the pretext of naming names was intended to close. In the course of this practice of unwitting contradiction, however, Skipper generates the laws of a new production, generated so that their intelligibility will be contingent upon the full complexity of their dissemination. Our ability to formulate these laws depends on our ability to recognize them as a condition of reading and not simply as an intrinsic principle of the character's fate. This, of course, presupposes a notion of formal integrity bound immediately within the processes of the text's production and not within the devices of genre control, which issue from ready-made categories of intelligibility.

The French theorist Pierre Macherey anticipates a means of regrounding the notion of generic form in his own efforts to define what we mean by that condition of "necessity" which circumscribes the text as a formal entity:

A condition is not that which is initially given, a cause in the empirical sense; it is the principle of rationality which makes the work accessible to thought. To know the conditions of a work is not to reduce the process of its production to merely the growth of a seed which contains all its future possibilities from the very beginning, a kind of genesis which is the reversed image of an analysis. To know the conditions of a work is to define the real process of its constitution, to show how it is composed from a real diversity of elements which give it substance.[11]

In *Second Skin*, the multiplication of contextual elements that constitute Skipper's narrative threatens to erode the very structures of coherence that make it a narrative, raising the issue of the work's formal integrity at the apparent limit of its intelligibility. The conflict between which kinds of knowledge a reader is prompted to seek by the text and which "principles of rationality" are evoked by the text (this conflict is the motor of every narrative) is more volatile in this fiction than in most other novels. For here the insufficiency of the narrative's forms of coherence to the readers' expectations is precisely a function of the text and not a factitious discrepancy between text and reader. The more Skipper's narrative insists upon subordinating the proliferating particulars of his story to the dichotomy of imagination and reality, evil versus good, the more unstable the dichotomy becomes. The more inclusive Skipper insists this structure is, the more contradictory it becomes. Thus, at the supposed climax of the novel, Tremlow appears to be simultaneously the touchstone of Skipper's experience of violation and a violation of the dichotomous rule that his experience invokes. Ultimately, the mutinous Tremlow, "that devil" (57), comes to personify the very gap between names and their referents, words and things, which necessarily results, as we know from Freud, in the overdetermination of the signifier.

Recounting Tremlow's mutiny, Skipper's consciousness echoes with the memory of all the other violations of his life. He is clearly engaged in the recuperative strategy of conventional trope, attempting to stabilize his identity by organizing the separate moments of his life under the authority of a single act of "naming." The laconic title of the chapter that dramatizes this "naming" is "The Brutal Act." In fact, three brutal acts are disclosed: Tremlow's mutiny, Skipper's father's suicide, and Skipper's son-in-law's murder. Each is mirrored in the single glass of the title as if to abstract the events into a harmonious allegorical register. Each ostensibly is a "type" of an original act of violence: Skipper's rape. Nevertheless, in the midst of this feat of naming, there erupts the revelation of Tremlow's Christian name— Harry. A devastating confusion ensues between the identity of the mutineer and a martyred sailor who Skipper learns gave his own life for Skipper's lost son-in-law, Fernandez. In the Second Avenue flophouse where Skipper discovers the bodies of Fernandez and Fernandez's mysterious angel of mercy, he scrupulously avoids contact with the martyr's face. While Skipper knows the name is identical to that of the mutinous Tremlow, the sailor's act of self-sacrifice actually denotes the role Skipper has chosen for himself. He is acutely aware that the contradiction of finding both roles incarnate in the same person would be overwhelming. He must suppress a potential insight into the inadequacy of a name to the circumstances it invokes, especially when the name depends for its lucidity upon a clearly articulated dialectic of opposites. The name dislocated from its fixed signified would jeopardize the stability of the language that ordains it and the world that language projects.

In its nominalistic purity as a self-announced *dénouement*, this plot episode conspicuously promises a *catharsis*: the reduction of all contradictions to a single moment of insight. But betrayed as it is by the unmanageable duplicity of the name (Harry), the episode demands a new set of formal expectations for reconciling the expressive power of language with the ambiguity of its existential pretexts. Therefore, it is necessary to explore the rhetorical basis of the epistemological crisis foregrounded in "The Brutal Act" before detailing its dramatic content.

III

By the contradictory force of their syntactical deferrals and contextual leaps, Skipper's locutions consistently guide the reader away from the horizon of contextual closure, taunting his expectation of formal *catharsis*. While Skipper's intentions seem deeply implicated in the teleology of naming, the very verbal process that seems to mobilize these intentions entails a teleologically abortive complexity. An example is Skipper's metaphorical apostrophe to the wind, which at first seems to follow a model of conventional trope. Its implicit mode is the logic of analogy or translation. Here, however, the lucidity of naming is dependent upon displacement of the object that prompts it.

But the wind, the bundle of invisible snakes, roars across our wandering island—it is a wandering island—of course unlocated in space and quite out of time—and seems to heap the shoulders with an armlike weight, to coil about my naked legs and pulse and cool and caress the flesh with an unpredictable weight and consistency, tension, of its own. These snakes that fly in the wind are as large around as tree trunks but pliant as the serpents that crowd my dreams. So the wind nests itself and bundles itself across this island, buffets the body with wedges of invisible but still sensual configurations. It drives, drives even when it drops, down, fades, dies, it continues its gentle rubbing against the skin. (46)

The organizing trope seems to analogize the wind with snakes. But the features of the wind are not succinctly anatomized by the metaphor. Nor are the points of resemblance between wind and reptile made explicit enough to collapse the terms of one experience into the other as its authoritative ground. On the contrary, instead of imposing a measure of logical closure upon the metaphoric tenor, the vehicle complicates it with new articulations. Furthermore, the attempt to represent the intangibility of the wind (a familiar rationale of figurative excursus) in concrete terms is revealed to be most fruitful in its tacit admission of failure.

If we look for a thematic rationale for these apparent inconsistencies, we find that the wind that breathes life into the idea of Catalina Kate's island—"it is a wandering island"—seems intended to provoke an explicit contrast with the wind that lashes Miranda's perversely named "gentle island" in the next episode of the novel. The contrast appears to be informed by the life-death, imagination-reality dichotomy. Miranda's "black" island is the scene of Cassandra's death. Kate's "golden" island will bear fruits of Skipper's love. Nevertheless, the eloquence of the quoted passage lies not in the reification of this dichotomous logic but in its own troping of the trope: Skipper's impulse toward invidious comparison. The imagistic deployment of this passage, like the wind it apostrophizes, scatters contextual parameters and alters the relevant patterns of relatedness. While the reptilian figure weaves through the passage, restating itself as if to confirm a single contextual imperative, each circuitous restatement engenders new possibilities that do not dispose themselves along the same logical/semantic axis of the fiction. The wind entangles Skipper in treacherous toils of its own volition; it by turns is as large as trees and as light as birds. Fittingly, this series of displacements climaxes with a discharge of sexual connotations that reflect the wind's own verbal genesis. The wind's "gentle rubbing against the skin" tropes the fertile friction of contextual edges that sustain it. Ironically, the figure of the snakes, apparently chosen to fix the wind as a signifier, unfolds as a commentary on the unfixedness of these signifying relations except as they convey reflexive knowledge about the text. Finally, it is not a natural resem-

blance between the reptile and the wind that is foregrounded
by the language of this passage but rather the text's demon-
stration of its own potential for new combinatory strategies.
Paradoxically, this passage as a whole turns out to be the most
persuasive metaphor for the wind by its very refusal to yield
a finite set of defining characteristics. A double structure of
meaning is implicit in this paradox, a structure which is instrumental to the narrative authority in this fiction and is nowhere
more explicit than in the systematic recurrence of reptilian imagery throughout.

The double structure is elucidated when we consider how
Skipper takes the reptile to be a totem for his personal experience of violation. Skipper struggles to preserve the iconic
status of the reptilian figure amidst the shifting contextual
markers that ultimately erode its denominative authority. The
repetition of the reptilian imagery precipitates a conflict that is
analogous to the duplicity of Tremlow's name, where repetition
breeds difference. I would designate the discursive level formed
in Skipper's desire to determine the symbolic value of the reptile as a characterological level, insofar as it gives priority to
a finite set of predicates (the predicates of violation) to which
the text returns in other episodes. Cassandra's vengeful tattoo
traces the letters of Fernandez's name onto Skipper's breast
like "a green lizard [which] lay exposed and crawling on my
breast." The green monster rears its head again in the green
taffeta bow billowing up in the back of Cassandra's bright party
dress like the storm of sexual aggression that Skipper fears will
break upon their "gentle island." Tremlow's mutiny is suffered
by Skipper in the suffusion of an ominous green light. Even the
spectacle of Catalina Kate's pregnancy is crowned by the vigil
of a large green iguana. As I said, this pattern epitomizes the
characterological level by its ostensible predication of a single
set of conditions as a thematic imperative under which Skipper's actions are meant to be intelligible.

But the apparent stability of these conditions is conspicuously destabilized by its complicity in the elaborations of Skip-

per's narration/Hawkes's prose. The consequence is a dispersal of the significations apparently stabilized by the leitmotif. This dispersal infers a supplementary, rather than a complementary, authorial level in the discursive structure of the book. With the designation of an authorial level I do not mean to posit a remote Joycean god of creation but rather a range of imaginative contingencies that on the one hand announce the possibility for recovering an already constituted meaning (fate, identity) through repetition and on the other pose an impassable obstacle to that end. The conflict displayed by this distinction dramatizes a dynamic relationship of author and character that, in the Lukácsian model of narrative, would be disguised by the ironic distance between character and plot predicates. In Lukács, the adequacy of characters to teleology is indexed as their fate, not as the language choices they embody.[12] The ironic perspective fostered in an omniscient, ironic text entertains apparent differences in order to reveal their hidden identity as a function of a privileged category of experience. For example, in a fiction like Dickens's *Hard Times*, a rich tapestry of social particulars is ultimately intelligible insofar as the contradictory fates of the characters sustain the opposition of Gradgrindian fact and circus illusion. The characters are predicated synecdochically in relation to an inclusive principle of identity. Thus they convey their meaning in a virtual tautology.

Hawkes appears to tease the same prospectus for the reader within Skipper's dichotomous ethos of victim-victimizer. But the difference is that in *Second Skin* the dichotomy itself succumbs as the target of the author's parodic aptitude. Contrary to the ironist's exploitation of difference as a vehicle for unifying predicates, Hawkes employs surface repetition (evident in Skipper's rhetorical invocation of the wind) as a vehicle for exposing intrinsic differences. Repetition invokes the model of conceptual stability as the object of scrutiny and hence as a suitable vehicle for self-consciousness. Thus, recurrent imagery functions as a virtual cause of authorial self-consciousness.

The rhythm of recurrence in *Second Skin* engenders a dissonant counterpoint: every repetition entails a syntactical elaboration that destabilizes the meaning relations it seems to represent. The sliding of contextual markers in the prose of this novel may now be judged to mime the duplicity of names that challenged the stability of Skipper's world in the first place. This rhetorical practice posits the authorial level as a kind of sympathetic magic transforming the effects of characterological fate within a new textual integrity. This rhetorical slippage illuminates the authorial level not as a simple allegorical representation of a purported past or as its dialectical alterity: rather, it is an elaboration that repeats, preserves, and surpasses the characterological or plot level. What we must take as an artifact of authorial presence in the contextual dissociations of the metaphoric vehicle is nonetheless projected from narrative devices that represent the perspective of the first-person narrator as an authorial perspective as well.

I have said that the superimposition of one contextual field upon another implicit in Hawkes's rhetoric frees the authority of the first person from the structures of coherence that nominally control it. Skipper stands both inside and outside his own narration because the narrative does not sustain a simple structural dichotomy. Furthermore, because metaphoric extension effects a transformation of the rules of exchange upon which contextual logic is founded, we can understand the characterological level to be directly constitutive of the authorial level. The authorial level itself articulates the limit of the characterological level with the built-in contingencies of its own ways of knowing. One level does not simply stand in an ironic ratio with respect to the incompleteness of the other. Their intelligibility is not the immanent complementarity of the pieces of a puzzle. Perhaps Hawkes is attracted to the first-person narrator precisely because it is an elegant metaphor for the author's relationship to his or her productions. The first-person narrator allows the author to confront the means of narrative production by dramatizing the crisis of a narrator torn between the fate he records and the immediate exigencies of authorship

that must stand as a denial of fate if they are to result in credible creations.

The problematic acknowledged here is most insistent in the very exclusivity of the first-person narrator as Hawkes employs it. But the implications of this formal structure can be understood more fully if we realize that the coincidence of authorial and characterological levels along a single axis of dissociation and displacement has a striking analogy in the theory of contemporary psychoanalysis.

In Jacques Lacan's controversial rereading of Freud, as it is was discussed in the last chapter, the subject is engendered within a notion of desire that is independent of any definite satisfactions.[13] In other words, desire denotes a signifier unbound by a unique signified. Desire therefore finds its clearest articulation within the rupture of contextual predicates. For John Hawkes—particularly when he speaks as the polemicist of a disruptive antirealist fiction—the cultural narcissism implicit in the forms of genre control incites a subjective anxiety/desire that cannot be discharged except by a deliberate violation of the medium that expresses it.

Hawkes expresses a desire to be simultaneously within and without the language, for his rhetoric opens a gap within the proairetic codes of conventional fiction that would otherwise denote an axiomatic combinatory logic. As I have suggested, this "opening" is mirrored in the paradox of a first-person narrator who suppresses all external perspectives yet does not ordain, even in his tyrannical control of point of view, a commanding center to which all the constituent parts are systematically subordinated. The blatant inscription of the proairetic codes within Skipper's dichotomous schematization of reality displays the parodic motive behind Hawkes's rhetorical manipulations. This schematization, though it serves as the vehicle of narrative authority, also serves as the vehicle for the discredit of its own authority. While the ironic use of conventional omniscient narrative binds a narrative to an already constituted authoritative perspective, parody presents the contrast of an expanding

frame of reference, the authority for which is projected outward rather than buried in the invisible depths of an abstract
interiority. In *Second Skin*, the syntactical suspense, the
anaphoric divagations, and the leitmotifs that do not return the
reader to the contextual source of their imagery bear the burden of Hawkes's parodic antirealism; all effect a reformulation
of the rules of contextual logic.

In contemporary psychoanalysis, the desires that form the
subject are similarly based on a dispossession of the fullness of
the signified. According to Lacan, language, like desire, stands
in the place of the "other." The other illuminates the situation of
the subject precisely because the subject is conceived not as an
entity but as a process of language acquisition. Acquisition
of the signifier, following Freud's description of the Fort/Da
game, is said to proceed by a splitting of the subject. This splitting (*spaltung*) is precipitated by the lack that recognition of
otherness implies.[14] Nevertheless, identification of the desire
structure that forms the subject is not a question of finding an
object adequate to its lack. Lacan locates its dynamic within
the child's dependency on the mother's body. The experience of
otherness originates in the mother's intermittent absences
from the child. Desire is founded in those bodily needs, such as
oral satisfaction, that are articulated as a demand for love. Demand constitutes the knowledge that satisfaction is situated in
the other. Lacan specifies that in the experience of the infant,
the particularity of demand is "articulated in the unconditionality of the demand for love" since particular satisfactions
(such as the need for food) do not satisfy the infant's multiplicity of needs. Therefore a metonymic residue always results
when the immediate motive of the demand for love is removed;
"desire is neither the appetite for satisfaction, nor the demand
for love but the difference that results from the subtraction of
the first from the second, the phenomenon of their splitting."[15]
The production of the subject occurs under the pressure of the
otherness that is not captured but rather articulated in a liber-
ating displacement. Significantly, Lacan links this dynamic of

articulation with the transformational and substitutive faculty of metaphor.

John Hawkes's dispersive deployment of the first-person narrator (dramatizing the conflict between the desire to tell and the desire not to be "told" by his own history) suggests the relevance of the psychological model to a fuller understanding of the expressive resources of the genre. For the split between the predicates that serve to authorize the narrator and the disruptions that mark authorial presence in *Second Skin* suggests that the production of meaning is a contingency of otherness. The novelist accedes to meaning or constitutes himself as a viable subject when he or she no longer depends upon the illusion of self-presence fostered within a representationally naive system of language. Naive representational language is deprived of rhetorical status until it is put into doubt, and this entails a willful duplicity of point of view or a displacement of narrative authority.

Commenting on the composition of *Second Skin*, Hawkes forcefully conveys his conviction that a conscientious duplicity is instrumental to fictive invention: "For me, the writer of fiction is his own angleworm and the sharper the barb with which he fishes himself out of the darkness, the better."[16] For Hawkes, the authorial function is inextricable from a self-contesting pragmatic, not unlike the solution to the Oedipal crisis that the child discovers in the exchange of being for having.[17] For the author seeking to substitute knowledge for self-possession, this exchange is linked to a deliberate realization of self-lack. Unlike the Oedipal child sacrificing the illusion of presence for the power of difference, the novelist sacrifices the illusion of the autonomy of representational language (which fixes the subject in the conventional discourse of the genre) for the greater mobility that is available for writer and reader alike within the codes they mutually inhabit.

At this point it makes deliciously perverse thematic sense to talk about the Oedipal exchange and Hawkes's use of metaphor in the terms of one of Lacan's most interesting commentators,

Alphonse De Waelhens, who equates metaphor with a process of mourning lost presence.[18] After all, Skipper's narrative is most emphatically mourning a host of lost relations. The victimized self that was constituted in their living relation to Skipper is more powerfully reconstituted in his act of talking about them. In his study of schizophrenia, De Waelhens argues that to be a sane person is preeminently to be able to insert one's self into the world of language, to escape the solipsistic bodily confinements of a mortal life by comprehending the metaphorical dimension of language.[19] Skipper's mourning, on a thematic level, is therefore caught in the meshes of an antithematic rhetoric evoking in its turn a Lacanian deconstruction of the model of egocentric subjectivity upon which all thematic reading subsists.

In the next chapter I will relate how this notion of the metaphoric capacity of the subject leads us to contemplate the subject's relation to reality. For now, the emphasis must return to the tension between thematic and rhetorical structures which Hawkes's own metaphoric strategy mightily sustains.

IV

I have suggested that "The Brutal Act" in *Second Skin* marks the maximal tension between thematic and rhetorical structures. For this reason, it is important to understand how this tension is resolved without on the one hand capitulating to the closure of ideological entrapment or, on the other, inducing a chaotic instability of meaning that subverts the formal integrity of the text itself. I have said that in "The Brutal Act" Hawkes has contrived a meticulous parody of novelistic *dénouement* by displaying its complicity in the psychological model of neurosis and the curative scene of recognition. After all, the first three-quarters of Skipper's narration in the book is sustained by a suspenseful deferral of Tremlow the mutineer and the revelation of the primal scene that Skipper sees mirrored in all the succeeding moments of violation. Out of his genealogical certainty he seeks to draw his self-justification.

The prospect of such a scenic *catharsis* alerts us to the possibility of a climactic unraveling of Skipper's fate from within, as though we could plumb a mysterious depth for a definitive measurement. Yet while "The Brutal Act" specifically names Skipper's gang rape by the villainous mutineers of the USS *Starfish* and therein suggests a scene of recognition that would ascertain identity and discover (for a reader) the missing center of the novel, the rape is the single action in the chapter that is not specifically named. The descriptive language enunciating the act itself is conspicuously evasive, displaced into peripheral imagery and indirect voicings of violence. Language masks a dramatic content that is otherwise meant to serve as the ultimate authorization of Skipper as character and narrator.

> the cloth ripping away from my flesh as if they were running the tip of a hot wire down the length of my thigh . . . And then "Dear God" I said but this too was merely a quick sensation deep in the heart because the grass skirt—wet, rough, matting of cruel grass—was rammed against me and there was only darkness and a low steady fatigued scuffling sound in the bottom of the white lifeboat along with my last spent cry of pain. (147)

Because the metaphor of the hot wire is not contextually primed by a clear exposition of the physical action, it lacks the epistemological stability of a legitimating tenor and, like the rest of the passage, speaks for absence rather than fullness of meaning. The burden of contextualization falls heavily on the reader. The impulse to contextualize is directed beyond the strictly circumscribed dramatic content of the novel to its linguistic apparatus.

The suspense of this episode is intelligible in Skipper's desire to capture the "true tonality" of his past and thereby to redeem the apparent irrationality of his lifelong victimization. Like any good narrative artist, he must show adequate cause in this "original" encounter between good and evil. With the touch-

stone phrase of this chapter—"shadings of the true tonality"—
Skipper passionately seeks an identity between the language
that marks him as narrator and the events that articulate his
personality. If successful, this identity would authorize a totalizing premise sufficient to the diversity of actions, signifying his
martyrdom throughout the novel. The execution of this chapter
is parody, precisely because in its ultimate inconclusiveness as
plot *dénouement* it does not simply present the catalytic moment of Skipper's life trauma but confronts it with its own facticity as *dénouement qua dénouement*.

"The Brutal Act" thus unfolds in a concatenation of metaphoric substitutions for the first authenticating moment of violence that transpired aboard the *Starfish*. The three disparate
moments of time marked by these substitutions, which succeed
one another without narrative transitions, superficially suggest
the thematic unification of conventional trope because they are
linked by a principle of resemblance—they are all archetypal
acts of violence dramatizing the dialectic of victim and victimizer. But while the iconic violence of the rape is repeated in
Skipper's memory of Fernandez's murder and his father's suicide, the causal logic denoted in the melodramatic timing of
Tremlow's appearance in the narrative is nullified by the very
overdetermination of meaning such plot manipulation is intended to repress. A *dénouement* that disperses rather than
recovers scenic content jeopardizes the entire structure it is
presumed to focus. Indeed, the enunciation of a strict, singleminded causality is crucial to Skipper's narrative. What is at
stake in the elaborate topos of the rape (and, like the leitmotif
of the green reptile, the act of violence repeats itself for Skipper in the ordeal of the tattooing, the belly-bumping contest,
the vigil of the iguana, the hissing soldiers who attack Skipper
and Cassandra in the desert) is the status of the victim. The
cathartic recognition of original evil promised in all that leads
up to "The Brutal Act" should, by locating a determinate center
of Skipper's experience, fix the signifying relations of the narrative and stabilize its meaning. Therefore, the text's betrayal

of this prospect for closure, implying an unprecedented mobility of the narrating subject, strikes at the heart of narrative authority and its traditional promise of continuity, closure, identity.

The crisis of this chapter, then, is the crisis of Skipper's own subjectivity. After all, the scenes that trope the rape are morally ambiguous tableaus—anathema to the dichotomous purity of the narrative logic that has projected Skipper's character to this point. The first tableau, the Second Avenue flophouse, qualifies Skipper's narcissistic obsession with his own victimization by refusing to disentangle the fate of the victim from the victimizer. The second tableau is the chronologically prior memory of Skipper's own childhood self detonating the bullet of his father's suicide. Both of these brutal acts, by engendering a sense of guilt and complicity, brutally violate the ethos of victimization that Skipper's narrative is otherwise bound to affirm.

For these reasons, we must look for the consequential action of this crucial chapter not in the representations of violence that give it structural lucidity, but in the rhetorical ambiguity that confuses the identities of Tremlow the villain, Harry the victim, and Skipper's father, the suicidal mortician. This confusion induces internal contradictions that are not automatically resolved by an external synthetic perspective. Nevertheless, amidst this confusion a means exists for locating meanings that are constructed in otherwise devastating contradictions of the chapter. These meanings are linked to the productive processes of the fiction.

The confusion is perpetrated by a now-familiar parodic structure of repetition that characteristically posits a shattering difference rather than invoking unifying likeness. Three chapters earlier, after the abortive Christmas Dance, Skipper confesses to Cassandra his knowledge of Fernandez's victimization and asks her to reconsider their mutual judgment of his villainy. Cassandra, the namesake of fate, takes Fernandez as the token of her own victimization, just as Skipper takes Tremlow as his. But in the earlier scene Skipper insists: "We were wrong about

him weren't we? Just a little, I think so Cassandra." This question recurs in the narrative of "The Brutal Act" after Skipper's
meticulous re-creation of the flophouse scene. But our recognition of the scene he describes is now charged with the new
knowledge of Tremlow's double lying at its center, a sign of its
volatile ambiguity. The repetition of the question—"We were
wrong about him weren't we?"—is typical of the compositional
strategies of this chapter insofar as it serves as a vehicle for
temporal displacement. Specifically, the question marks the
threshold between the scene of Fernandez's murder and Skipper's father's suicide. But the signal recurrence of the question
as a motor for transition even more conclusively typifies the
contradictory logic to which a reader must adapt in order to
make this novel whole. In "The Brutal Act," the pronoun—"We
were wrong about *him*"—posits a dual reference at the same
moment that it moves the reader across the threshold of a new
temporal perspective. In its original context (Skipper's confession of Fernandez's death), "him" displayed the unreasonable
coincidence of victimizer and victim in the person of Fernandez.
This implicitly cast doubt on Skipper's nominalistic grasp of reality. But here that ambiguity is itself conspicuously troped by
the immediate contextual relevance of the reference to Tremlow as well as to Fernandez.

For Skipper to admit being wrong about Tremlow, he must
radically suspend the predicative authority that anchors his
narrative. Such an admission concedes a slippage between sign
and signified that jeopardizes the sense-making authority of
characterological predicates. Nonetheless, while the first-person
narrator is unconscious of the duplicity of the pronominal reference, it coincides with another temporal displacement of the
narrative. Thus, by projecting the reader into the scene of the
father's suicide, the narrative *effects* an insight into the mobility
of subjective positions to which the narrator himself is oblivious.
That is, the displaced temporality—because it is coincident
with our recognition of the limit of characterological knowledge—thus traces a perimeter of contextual exteriority that

opens the scenic content upon divergent syntactical paths. This chapter focuses discursive meaning like a telescopic eye opening one perspective on the perimeter of another. But because the insufficiency of the characterological logic here is captured in the emergent possibilities for new contextual combinations, it does not yield the usual ironies—those that disjoin character from an omniscient totalizing perspective subordinating the imaginary to the real, the figural to the literal. In another kind of novel, the internal contradictions of this chapter might tend to discredit the narrator. We could then explain the contradictions as the "return of the repressed" or merely the identity of a neurotic personality.[20] On the contrary, these contradictions preclude the knowledge that would release character from the process of narrative language that begets it.

In the transformational character of this chapter, the text demonstrates its own means of production, articulating the contradictions that traverse its discourse as new combinatory possibilities. Of course, within this frame of reference, the object of representation focused by this fiction is not a unified consciousness but rather the process of consciousness embodying new forms of relatedness. Skipper is never simply displaced by the contradictions that seem to divide his discourse against itself. He is reconstituted in these differences as the agent of an emergent perspective. The contextual imperative of this writing—like the formation of the subject in psychoanalysis—is linked to a contradictory outside to which the signifier must refer in order to signify at all. The significance of this exteriority is made more explicit in the final transformation of this chapter, as the scene of Fernandez's martyrdom turns into the scene of Skipper's complicity in his father's death. The simultaneity of the Oedipal trauma (the father's suicide) with the author's violation of the fathering devices of narrative reminds us that Hawkes is self-consciously in conflict with the authorizing devices that inhibit the authorial imagination. Perhaps this is the ultimate parodic gesture that implicates this narrative in the furtive polemic of all Hawkes's fiction: "plot, character, setting, and theme are the enemies of the novel."

If any conventional narrative ironies appear in the wake of this chapter, they are not generated out of the subjectivity of Hawkes's first-person narrator. Rather, they spring from expectations of readers for whom—to use Roland Barthes's formulation—narrative convention "depends upon inscription of the subject as the place of intelligibility."[21] An intelligibility inscribed as a prior perspective of meaning is precisely what is displaced in Hawkes's fiction. This makes it as difficult for the reader to find him- or herself in the text as to fix Skipper's identity as the manipulator of codes of readability. Nevertheless, by putting the subject in process/crisis, the destabilizations in this novel do not nullify intelligibility. Rather, by dissolving fixed positions of signification, the text re-presents them as new objects whose very conditionality informs the possibility of self-renewal that they denote. The rape returns in successive scenes of violence that Skipper accepts as confirmation of his own identity but that at the same time will not be disposed along the single axis of meaning which that identity denotes. Indeed, we have seen how the parodic reflexiveness of this fiction sustains itself by refinding its discursive material as the same but different, thus dramatizing the interplay between the narrating subject (Skipper) and the ways of knowing that express him.

V

Formally, Hawkes's novel resembles an insubordinate metaphor, a catachresis that sets contextually incommensurate realities against one another so that the contradictions become the terms of new creation. Likewise, in the specific density of its metaphoric rhetoric, the novel proclaims its own object to be the renewal of signifying positions. Like the structure of conventional metaphoric trope, the authority of the proper name upon which this fiction's first-person narrator presumes is a question no longer of the disposition of objects with respect to a subject, but rather of the very process of the subject's desire for expression.

In *Second Skin*, then, events are not as important as the

modes of knowledge that operate them. Through the eyes of Hawkes's polemical persona, it is easy to see that the essential epistemological work of the genre might indeed be parody. This mode recognizes the essential secondariness of literary language to be the access to imaginative power, not an imposing obstacle to it. In this recognition, the novelist unburdens her- or himself of that hypostasis of subjective positions that haunts the genre in the guise of the real. Hawkes purges this ghost of narrative authority in the transformation of his narrative beyond the means of its authorizing predicates.

In the final chapter of *Second Skin*, the name bestowed on Catalina Kate's newborn child has meaning not as it specifies identity but rather as it enables the fathering of new positions for a signifying subject. In the cemetery where the child is baptized, Skipper asks: "Who do you think he looks like, Kate? Sonny or me?" Catalina Kate answers, almost as though out of the experience of reading this novel, "Him look like the fella in the grave." Identity and life are bred in contradictions like those forming the subject in the Lacanian theory of language. Correspondingly, what began as a fiction of intentions predicated on recovery of the past (a project bound within the modes of knowledge that enunciate it) ends by reconciling the sincerity of intention with the facticity of composition. Hawkes meticulously works this ending with a language that refuses to discharge the effect of closure, which its content so clearly proffers:

> Because now I am fifty nine years old and I knew I would be and now there is the sun in the evening, the moon at dawn the still voice. That's it. The sun in the evening. The moon at dawn. The still voice. (210)

Skipper's age certainly does not authenticate the meaning of the preceding narrative chronologically. The past—an acknowledged burden of this narrative—is collapsed into a dynamic present in much the way that conventional codes of this fiction are reconstituted as a process of language at the apparent limit of formal autonomy.

I have written here that the rhetorical complexity of this novel pertains to the supplementarity of Hawkes's prose, dispersing the traditional categories of novelistic meaning and in that dispersal identifying the transitional faculty of language as the esthetic catalyst of the text. In the final paragraph of the novel, the paradoxical imagery of the sun in the evening and the moon at dawn suggests predication caught in the awareness that transition is its authentic condition. Furthermore, the absence of full predication in the closing sentence—"The still voice"—suggests the insufficiency of any hypostatized moment or meaning to the desire for self-expression activated in the device of the first-person narrator. This insufficiency is manifest throughout. The narrative of *Second Skin* subsists on contradictions that threaten its articulation as a coherent discourse. Indeed, the narrating voice may be seen as deconstructing its own enabling devices. But this deconstruction is not anarchically free of sense-making imperatives. The "name" (device) of the first-person narrator is disseminated through the contextual flux of the novel until the only sufficient account of its true reference is the totality of the conflicts displayed within it. Skipper's voice is therefore identifiable with the constitutive power of metaphor in Hawkes's novel.

We have contrasted the conventional recuperative trope with Hawkes's destabilizing trope, so we may contrast the peculiar representational project of this novel with that more familiar and more naive mimesis that ingenuously blinds itself to the fact that linguistic mediation is the infrastructure of even the most austere realism. In its presumption to recover a lost presence, naive representational art must always hear the hollowness of its own claims reverberate as a devastating irony rather than sound the keynote of its own self-sustaining powers of imagination. That Hawkes takes his own awareness of this mediation to be the threshold of invention is clear. The naive allegory of authorship evoked by the trappings of first person is put decisively under the sign of death. The parodic reflexiveness of this gesture richly accords with Roland Barthes's well-known analysis of novelistic realism.

> The Novel is a Death; it transforms life into destiny, a memory into a useful act, duration into orientated and meaningful time. But this transformation can be accomplished only in full view of society. It is society which imposes the Novel, that is, a complex of signs, as a transcendence and as the History of a duration. It is therefore by the obviousness of its intention, grasped in that of the narrative signs, that one can recognize the path which, through all the solemnity of art binds the writer to society.[22]

Hawkes will not submit to this death. Indeed, Hawkes's polemical endorsement of the criminal act and the antirealist practice of his fiction are linked in the knowledge that the novelist must murder the institutional forces that conspire in his or her own authorship. Hawkes's antirealism paradoxically jeopardizes the lucidity of the genre and renews its meaning.

I began this chapter by remarking that for the novelists of renunciation, expression is always paradoxical. The imaginative will, struggling to express itself through enabling devices that propel an obstinate otherness, succeeds only in expressing the forms of its own desire.

Contrast this version of novelistic form with Henry James's caveat that the form of the genre lies in the determinations of a "commanding center." In the preface to *The Ambassadors*, James deplores the use of the first-person narrator because it admits "scant exposure to criticism."[23] In James's fiction, of course, "criticism" authenticates external perspectives afforded by expository devices like the *ficelle*. These techniques of characterization focus the commanding center of the work through their own complementarity with it. Hawkes's use of the first person is distinguished by the fact that such "external" points of view are attributable to the center-subject-narrator as internal contradictions appearing to destroy egocentric desire. Skipper's name is a perfect exemplum. For "Skipper" denotes both the authoritarian helmsman of this text and the parodic diminutive given as a nickname to children: an ironic comment on their powerlessness. It is a noun *and* a verb; he is author and character, victim and victimizer. The name is a source of predication in language as it is of knowledge in the novel. But in *Second Skin*, the name is not simply a means of authenticating the subject according to a proprietary rule. It is a way of inhabiting the imaginative possibilities that the proprietary rule excludes. The name is a means of mobilizing identity across the threshold of its production. The effect is to dispel the illusion of the autonomous lucidity of conventional meaning. This understanding of names becomes a constitutive insight of the genre as Hawkes conceives it. The name-bearing character is not simply an object of language in Hawkes's novel. Character is absorbed by language. The representation of the desire of the authorial will is not the default of some other project of representation, but the only project to which the desire to represent is clearly adequate.

This does not mean that the first person in Hawkes's fiction is merely a site for infinite substitutions of identity. The ways of knowing that are shed in Skipper's narration are not discarded. They are renewed and reconstituted by the contextual transformations upon which the articulation of desire depends.

Finally, Hawkes's subject is freedom. The possible meanings that a subject is capable of disclosing are more important than a hypostatized logic of motivation or context. The novel, understood as Skipper understands his authorial role at the start of the novel (as a hypostasis of fixed relations of representation), is the victim of a deathly tautology. If we then take Hawkes's novel as a meditation on the life of the genre, we may conclude that the "criminal act" is the fiction writer's salvation because it acknowledges his or her own mediational status (vis-à-vis his own discourse) as the essential knowledge that the novel can uniquely grasp. Hawkes's criminal persona does not destroy but rather violates the authority of self as the only proper authorization of its productions.

The violation of the self, then, underlies my discussion of catachrestic metaphor in narrative. And, as we shall see in the next chapter, those artists who have chosen to contest the static authority of institutional language with the mobility of metaphor have already deeply implicated themselves in a rethinking of the Cartesian subject, which otherwise retains unquestioned sovereignty over the pronouncements of humanist art.

5
THE
NEED
OF
THE
PRESENT

HOW IT IS
WITH THE
SUBJECT IN
BECKETT'S NOVEL

What I am saying does not mean that there will
henceforth be no form in art. It only means that there
will be new form, and that this form will be of such a
type that it admits the chaos and does not try to say
that the chaos is really something else. The form and
the chaos remain separate. The latter is not reduced
to the former. That is why form itself becomes a
preoccupation because it exists as a problem separate
from the material it accommodates.

Samuel Beckett,
in "Beckett on the Madeleine,"
by Tom Driver

The pride of humanist art is an entrancing dream of order to
which we awaken from the chaotic tossings and turnings of existence. This artful somnambulism is induced by the painful
paradox of human consciousness, which has its most perspicuous and influential formulation in the Cartesian cogito: the mind
irremediably divided against itself. For Cartesian man, the life
of the mind is the lullaby of the body's deep sleep.

The art of Samuel Beckett has been honored as a most eloquent expression of the pathos of this consciousness. Beckett's

preoccupation with the Cartesian dilemma appears through a succession of quintessentially alienated personae. Their prophetic insights into the all too fathomable recesses of human consciousness cause them to endure eternal exile from the promised land of being. Self-consciousness banishes Beckett's characters to a reality deprived of a world. And yet, replete as Beckett's *oeuvre* is with sharp delineations of paradoxical self-consciousness, it is worth considering that Beckett's fiction has, as a result, been given too thoughtlessly to the services of a virtually omnipotent theme of modern art criticism: the absurdity of the human condition. The theme of man's absurdity too easily sublimates the disconcerting predicament of Cartesian consciousness into a solacing wisdom of the heart. The ironic passivity of this absurdist stance is belied in Beckett by a conspicuously active rhetorical density. While we feel an undeniably acute pang for the spiritual diaspora of modern cultural experience, Beckett's art nonetheless remains formally antagonistic to the dominant cultural generalizations about modern consciousness that seek to absolve us of the very experiential conflicts they display. Beckett's formal experiments thwart all aphoristic speculation that makes existential humanity's self-martyring self-consciousness merely a touchstone of nobility, merely another metaphorical restitution of the wholeness of the human universe.

The inadequacy of this fashionably ironic thematic gloss is perhaps clearest in the work of Martin Esslin, who asks the perennial question of Beckett criticism: "How is it that [his] vision of the ultimate void in all its grotesque derision and despair should be capable of producing an effect akin to the catharsis of great tragedy?"[1] By following a logic of paradoxical resemblance—a simple metaphoric reversal whereby despair is recast as knowledge, emptiness as fullness—Esslin predictably goes on to say: "the very act of confronting the void or continuing to confront it is an act of affirmation. . . . The uglier the reality that is confronted the more exhilarating will be its sublimation into symmetry, rhythm, movement and laughter."

In this analysis, the eloquence of Beckett's despair natural-
izes the very estrangement that is signified in its articulate
forms. And yet, the naturalizing, totalizing, inclusive logic imputed to the form of Beckett's work here is anathema to Beckett's own sobering esthetic prescription. The rhetorical fulcrum
of Beckett's dialogue with Tom Driver is his stipulation that the
"form and the chaos remain separate." While the latter is not
reduced to the former, the chaos is not "something else." These
statements sound an admonition against the familiar rational-
izations of metaphor, whereby the mind recovers the unfamiliar
to a category of familiar experience. On the contrary, in response to the critical consensus about his work, Beckett bluntly
retorts: "My work is a matter of fundamental sounds (no joke
intended) made as fully as possible, and I accept responsibility
for nothing else. If people want to have their headaches among
the overtones, let them. And provide their own aspirin."[2] If we
take this statement as anything more than an obligatory disclaimer of critical cant, we must admit an understanding of
Beckett's work that confronts the disjuncture between form
and meaning without ready-made apologies.

Characteristically the persona of Beckett's fiction appears to
unmask the face of experience by fastidiously divesting him- or
herself of the self-deluded disguises availed by expressionist
esthetics. Beckett's hostility toward expressionist theories of
art is well known. The text for this esthetic dictum is "Three
Dialogues with Georges Duthuit," a conspicuously fictionalized
document in which an assiduously characterized B. declaims:
"[For] the artist obsessed with his expressive vocation, anything and everything is doomed to become occasion."[3] Occasion
is linked with the goal of self-representation. Expression occa-
sions the recurrence of those modes of knowledge by which the
subject is manifested in his or her own discourse. As we shall
see, the mechanism of this recurrence is humanity's proclivity
toward narrative fulfillments of desire, toward finding paradoxical resemblances to unify the experience of diverse particulars. This is, of course, the appointed work of metaphor,

and it will lead us to question the rhetorical basis of literary production.

First, however, we must observe how curious it is that the avoidance of occasion in Beckett's theoretical perspective becomes the occasion for promulgating a theory of action. The manifest poverty of occasion in Beckett's terms is stasis. Action, its logical antithesis, offers a transformation of or a transition between different levels of experience and knowledge. But the curiosity of Beckett's enthusiasm for action is that it is nowhere to be found in the plots of his novels. Action is the impossible dream taunting Beckett's paralytic personae. Molloy cannot successfully act on the desire to regain his mother's house. Moran cannot fulfill his mission to locate Molloy. The Unnamable will never be able to contact his "master." The impossibility of action is in fact the obstacle to a conventional plot structure that would effect a strict teleological progress in Beckett's novels. Therefore, since the narrative situation of Beckett's heroes is always static, we must look for the *anagnorisis* or change of perspective—the means by which we register action in orthodox plot—not in the narrative event, but in the narrative gap. Before we can pursue this line of inquiry, however, we should first understand how Beckett means for us to redefine our terms—act, agent, action—so that they may be used to unravel such seemingly paradoxical claims.

The Dutch painter Bram Van Velde is the exemplar of the peculiar notion of action upon which Beckett's condemnation of the expressive occasion seems to rest:

> he is the first to accept a certain situation and to consent to a certain act. . . . The act is of him who helpless cannot paint, since he is obliged to paint. The act is of him who helpless, unable to act, acts in the event, paints since he is obliged to paint.[4]

Action here is divorced from intention, whereby events reduce to a privileged cause. For this reason, Beckett's concept of action is antithetical to the Aristotelian *mythos*, which scrupulously emphasizes means over ends, motive over act, and resolves the meaning of the events in a character's life within the univocal predicates of cathartic reversal. Oedipus is revealed to be the man he always was. Reversal in this scheme is always repetition. Insofar as the *mythos* of narrative is the incidence of a repetition, it is also the occasion of identity.

Here, then, we may begin to understand the basis of Beckett's objection to expression and hence his objection to familiar plot forms. For repetition-identity is the demon of Beckett's earliest speculation on the philosophical prospectus for narrative art in the twentieth century. Beckett's *Proust* is an acid remonstration against the inexorable logic of the habitual. He recognizes in the habitual a principle of causality based on resemblance, and on this basis he condemns it. The fruit of identifying disparate moments of experience in memory, that is, the quintessential habit of mind, is lamentably always a temptation toward a preemptive stasis and hence the nemesis of act. According to Beckett, only the moment that "inaugurates a transition" accedes to what Proust calls our "first nature" and posits action as viable creation. For Beckett this is the moment when

> the boredom of living is replaced by the suffering of being. . . . When [an] object is perceived as particular and unique and not merely the member of a family, when it appears independent of any general notion and detached from the sanity of a cause, isolated and inexplicable in the light of ignorance, then and only then it may be a source of enchantment. . . . Normally we are in the position of the tourist . . . whose esthetic experience consists of a series of identifications. . . . The creature of habit turns aside from the object that cannot be made to correspond with one or other of his intellectual prejudices."[5]

The transitional moment, however, seems to offer an action without an agent, thereby legitimating a dangerous threshold of disorder. In fact, Beckett's contempt for the "sanity of a cause" encroaches on that sacred repository of causal logic: the rational mind. It is an invitation to chaos. After all, the source of enchantment to which Beckett aspires in this passage is an extraordinary conceptual mobility—what Beckett elsewhere calls "the free play of every faculty." Such mobility is necessarily forfeited by that arbitrary reconciliation of form and chaos occasioned every time we rationalize the resemblance of cause and effect. Furthermore, that identity is precisely the sense-making burden of every expressive occasion for subjective consciousness. Not only does Beckett's repudiation of expression (that is, the causality imputed from resemblance) obviate a classical narrative teleology but, more important, it also calls into doubt the institution of subjectivity and the psychology upon which all action, dramatic and existential, is predicated as causal will or intention.

Nevertheless, let us be clear that for the purposes of this discussion, subjectivity is a locus of rationality and not the limit of rationality. Ratiocination in the absence of an intending subject to ground it engenders conflict and contradiction but not necessarily nonsense for an interpreting consciousness. The *aporia* of contradiction is after all the threshold of knowledge that Beckett's novels typically invite us to cross. In the monologues of Beckett's most notorious narrators, the meticulous self-scrutinizing catechism of narration results in a paradoxical displacement of the predicative agency that otherwise authorizes the discourse. The questions on the first page of *The Unnamable*, "Where now? Who now? What now?," are perfect phrasings of the problem Beckett poses for his reader: he announces in the "voice" of rational discourse the absence of an agent of discursive rationality. This is a founding absurdity of Beckett's work. The subject of rational discourse in Beckett's novels exists virtually as an absent cause denoted by a narrative structure for which the word "effect" no longer accords the certainty of definition. This problematic, I will argue, marks the significant formal innovation of Beckett's work. Furthermore, I will insist that its explication must devolve to rhetorical analysis.

Rhetoric is the index of subjective position and so apprehends the conceptual mobility to which Beckett aspires in his theoretical declarations. It is at this level of analysis that Beckett's esthetic is implicated in a praxis that is not narrowly literary but rather extends to the world of action. In *Proust*, Beckett asserts that "the artist is active." But as we will see, action, unlike expression, does not denote a logic of predictability or, as in the traditional novel, an enabling, ennobling *telos*. Action, distinguished from expression, entails a deliberate self-subversion that the Freudian egocentric subject does not have the power to ordain.

I

Paul Ricoeur's impressive anatomy of metaphor, *The Rule of Metaphor*,[6] has (as I have pointed out in earlier chapters) linked the change of meaning (*epiphora*) produced by trope with the artist's act of creation (*mimesis*), thus offering a rich context for a rhetorical analysis of the absent/present subject in Beckett's discourse. Ricoeur has made it possible to examine plot and narrative form in the terms of trope because he sees trope, like narrative, as a predicative phenomenon and not a phenomenon of denomination or substitution. Ricoeur's metaphor does not displace the lexical axis from the syntactical axis of language, as our orthodox rhetorical primers instruct. Metaphor produces a rearrangement of predicates, a transposition of categorical boundaries, tantamount to what Gilbert Ryle calls "category mistake." Ricoeur suggests that the category mistake is nothing more than "the complement of a logic of discovery" postulating new categorical priorities. This logic of discovery is the corollary to Beckett's subject-subverting notion of subjectivity.

In Beckett, the apparent elision of the category of the subject (evident in the disjunctures of causes and effects) presents an obstacle to our habits of reading novels. This disjuncture further disrupts the teleology of conventional narrative development, jeopardizing the formal coherence of the genre. Ricoeur reminds us that metaphor also possesses a teleological aspect in the principle of resemblance that operates the trope. While the celebrated *enargia* of Aristotle's metaphor is a disruptive violation of a paradigmatic order, the disruption is ultimately only apparent or provisional. Each choice of diction integrates a contextually harmonious series obedient to a prior rule of propriety or cause. Working on the Aristotelian hypothesis that *lexis* is rooted in *mimesis*, Ricoeur develops the idea that *lexis* and hence metaphor (the motor of lexical change) "exteriorizes and makes explicit the internal order of *mythos* or plot,"[7] thus linking *mimesis* to *mythos*. In the same argument, Ricoeur reminds us that the concept of *mimesis* must not be equated with the concept of copying, but rather with the act of making: "There is *mimesis* only where there is making."[8] At this point, Ricoeur is quite aware that a notion of creation based on a notion of resemblance results in a conceptually problematic understanding of artistic production. Since for Aristotle "one imitation is always of one thing,"[9] a discontinuity between the creator and the thing created must be postulated if we are to avoid a tautology. To put it another way, making that is not copying presupposes a discontinuity in the intentional structure of the act. Since *mimesis* is linked to metaphor, Ricoeur looks to metaphor for a schematic elucidation of this problematic and finds reason to revise the rhetorical tradition derived from Aristotle's *Poetics*.

As I have said, Ricoeur shows that metaphor is preeminently a violation of a taxonomic category, that is, a discontinuity. In this discontinuity lies its productive agency and its preeminence in classical tropologies. The rhetorical tradition out of Aristotle, however, teaches that the lexical deviation produced by metaphor is linked to the lexical item it replaces; if this is true, it is hard to conceive how metaphor creates new meaning in accordance with Ricoeur's thesis that metaphor is also productive. On the contrary, the strange term of metaphor would simply call back the elided "proper" word. The lexical deviation would revert to the status of an index. The readings that flow from such an understanding enforce the traditional oppositions between proper and figurative, ordinary and strange, orderly and transgressing. Ricoeur disputes this notion of trope because he seeks to destroy such oppositions, to break their hold on our thinking about the practice of *poesis*. They obscure the nature of *mimesis* because they postulate a disjuncture between the categorical restraints on meaning and the processes of language that produce categorical distinctions. These oppositions privilege a taxonomic order over a constitutive order.

As an alternative, Ricoeur offers an admittedly "venturesome" hypothesis: "If metaphor belongs to an heuristic of thought could we not imagine that the process that distorts a certain logical order, a certain conceptual hierarchy . . . is the same as that from which all classification proceeds?"[10] The creation of meaning by the construction of plots—that is, *mimesis*—is thus thought to be homologous with the structure of metaphoric trope. But by insisting on the statement-making or predicative character of metaphor, Ricoeur asserts that metaphor posits not a simple recombination of elements according to a preestablished hierarchy but rather a generative syntax revealing new combinatory possibilities, structuring relations out of difference rather than resemblance. Ricoeur's venturesome hypothesis has in common with the lexical code it disrupts not a categorical difference but rather the process of categorical differentiation itself. According to Ricoeur's understanding of metaphor, the second term or vehicle redistributes the predicates of Richards's putative "tenor" or first term; it does not hypostasize their relation. Metaphor precipitates a code change that is not recoverable to a prior discursive order. Ricoeur agrees with all readers of Aristotle that metaphor is a deviation of meaning; but for him the deviation occurs at the level of the lexical code as a whole, not at the contextual level, where the strange term, in isolation from the predicates it integrates, presents merely a "semantic impertinence."

In this reading of Aristotle, we can detect a paradox with a familiar ring, for Ricoeur's metaphor suggests a disruptive causality without a cause. Disruption refers us not back to the order it interrupts but forward to the order it creates. Metaphors are powerful not by their capacity to repeat or replicate the code but by their capacity to differentiate the relational structure of language.

Beckett's *How It Is*[11] offers particularly fertile ground for sowing the speculation of the past few pages. I choose what many readers consider to be Beckett's most hermetic formal experiment for two reasons that relate specifically to the rhetorical ground I have furrowed here. First, the organizational principle of the text is starkly syntactical, that is, predicative, not semantic. It therefore throws into relief the production of metaphor as a predicative phenomenon. Second, despite its avoidance of the devices of literary realism, the novel is conspicuously free of strategies of figuration associated with the complementary antirealist mode. Hence it lends itself to an analysis that supersedes both the thematic opposition of realism-antirealism and the related conceptual red herring that invidiously legitimates nonmimetic or antirepresentational art over the naive imitation of life presented by traditional forms. Along with Beckett, I am not concerned with the uses of form to render hypostatic unity or totalization of experience, realistic or not. As he stipulates, the preoccupation with form relates to the question of how it articulates, rather than solves, the problem it confronts. To sound the refrain of Beckett's antiexpressionism once again, the form and the chaos do not become the same thing. In other words, the contingencies of form are as significant as the purpose form gives to expression. I will show how Beckett's interest in the subject is likewise confined to the disclosure of the contingencies it expresses rather than to some hypostatic content. And this makes possible a conceptualization of the subject that is quite articulate with the act of creative imagination as Beckett has written about it.

II

In *How It Is*, Beckett confronts the problem of the subject as it appears in the guise of *telos*. The frustrated teleology of the narrative is nowhere more frustrating than in the title itself. The title *How It Is* enunciates a stubbornly, obdurately impersonal present-tense predication. As such, it remains aloof from those familiar critical interrogatives that unify novels by disposing the particulars of event and character to specific categories of resolution: Who is the agent? What is the action? What happens next? These questions appeal to a complex temporality (rendered irrelevant by Beckett's title) wherein past, present, and future integrate a deductive logic for the reading subject. It is precisely this deductive, causal logic that Beckett's rhetoric avoids.

And yet Beckett's narrator deliberately courts the logical expectations of this complex temporality by disposing the narrative into a strict Aristotelian tripartite structure: beginning, middle, end; time before Pim, with Pim, and after Pim. Multidimensional time solicits the human drama in its archetypal dimensions. In the time of the narrator's solitude, face down in the mud, Pim is his invocation to the muse, that is, the postulate of an existential "other" enabling the narrator's self-representation. Pim, the "other," serves the narrator as the point of reference whereby he can project a temporal perspective. Consequently, the movement and transition of the subject with respect to a fixed object will be causal.

Nevertheless, the full structural ramifications of the Pim-narrator agon suggest that a theory of the subject based on patterns of logical causality results in a naive understanding of intersubjectivity. The narrator's relationship with Pim is staged as a Pavlovian farce. The subject (cause) produces effects in the other that present the other as an objectification of the subject's will. Here is the protocol: nails in Pim's armpit produce song; blade in his arse produces speech; thump on the skull makes silence; and pestle on the kidney controls the volume. Pim's otherness in this way dictates a relation with the narrator that is inversely proportional to the narrator's own subjective positionality. Pim is an index of the narrator's subjectivity. Pim as the object of the narrator's desire lends purpose to the narrator's movement. In turn, the movements of the narrator acquire significance insofar as they constitute the object that traces his effect. It is perhaps more useful to put it in terms reminiscent of the exposition of metaphoric logic given in the previous pages and say that the object exists insofar as the effect names the cause.

This structural relation, reminiscent as it is of the logical form of denominative or name-transference metaphor (where the substituted name returns discourse to the proper lexical choice), makes it possible to construe Pim as a kind of metaphoric substitution for the narrator. On this basis, we see the relation as compatible with the logical form of a strict narrative teleology.

So far, the structure of *How It Is* presents an unproblematic representation of the subject as a monadic center. Nevertheless, I have called attention to the complicated tropology of narrator and object not because it is the determinate rhetoric of this fiction but because it is in turn troped by a reverse causality. Its very susceptibility to reversal hints at a rhetorical density radically incommensurate with the causality that we have been led prematurely to see as paradigmatic for this novel. While the narrator of *How It Is* meticulously orders the details of his life before Pim, with Pim, and after Pim, he nonetheless passionately protests that the words so ordered are not his own:

how it is, I wrote before Pim, with Pim After Pim, how it is three parts I say it as I hear it. (7)

Beckett's narrator scrupulously ascribes the cause of his speech to a higher cause in relation to which he is the obedient effect. The resultant transposition of cause and effect carries the force of a logical contradiction that disturbs the teleological certainty of the tripartite plot structure (the movement toward and away from Pim, but always centered on the narrator's being). After all, the narrator cannot be both cause and effect within the same hierarchy of priorities. What is needed is a way to integrate the two sets of priorities and embrace the contradiction within a teleology larger than Pim.

I have stressed a rhetorical analysis in this discussion of plot elements because rhetoric displays the mechanism whereby transformation of meaning occurs and contradiction is mollified by reason. In order to restore the contradicted subject to the unity upon which the expressive esthetic depends, we need a vehicle precisely for transition from one causality to another. Yet we shall see that the mediating power of conventional denominative trope is ultimately not adequate to the disjunctures of this fiction. I will show how, by supplying a transition from one causality to another in accordance with the analogical logic of denominative metaphor, Beckett's narrator is led into a contradictory perspective that parodies and supersedes the expressive function we hold sacred in the unity of first person.

But first we must be guided by the expectations of a more naive tropology. The voice within quotation marks is characterologically the voice of self-doubt perpetually on the brink of withdrawing its predications ("Something wrong there . . .") in order to escape the oblivion of contradiction. Identity decrees noncontradiction. The narrator's authority within the scenic horizon of "vast tracts of time" is dependent on his ability to devise a structural order enabling him to distinguish the otherwise indistinguishable and hence interminable moments of his life: hence he will bring a compelling end to an otherwise infinite series. The adequacy of the end term, specifically designated as "Part Three After Pim," depends on its degree of congruence with the other parts, so that no particulars in the narrative remain unsubordinated or unassimilated to its meaning. Unmediated particulars appear as conspicuous difference. Obtrusive differences posit contradictory ends and defer the closure upon which the narrator stakes his credibility as a subjective consciousness.

Recognizing the formal constraints under which narrative desire is expressed in *How It Is*, we can now say that the narrator's hypothesis of the prior—that is, timeless—voice appears as a deliberate compensation for the contradictions that the experience of real time must breed in any human life. This "master voice" suggests a causality that brings an unstable heterogeneity neatly under the sign of a privileged homogeneity. In this way, Beckett elicits a dynamic of resemblance and contradiction (again morphologically related to denominative metaphor) that balances the otherwise discontinuous levels of utterance/quotation. Indeed, the relation of the quotational voice and the narrator ("I say it as I hear it") with the narrator and Pim presents the form of a proportional metaphor: A:B:C:D. This multipart trope, as we have seen in Ricoeur's analysis of denominative metaphor, postulates creation of meaning in terms of reproduction of the conditions of meaning. One set of terms is justified by its reduction to the code of another.

And yet, even as the trope is articulated we are alert to its inadequacy; undeniably it is a parodic echo of Christian theology's analogy explaining the relation of the unique creator of the world to that creation: God is to humanity as humanity is to the remembered moments of time. The analogy is an apposite expository device here since the contradictoriness to be avoided by Beckett's narrator, like the confusing manifold of existence that humans must escape to prevent the endless dispersion of self in time, demands a threshold of transcendence. Inasmuch as the theological figure offers a solution to the problem of the one and the many, Beckett's metaphorical "voice" seems clearly designed to reconcile the narrator broken in time (and thus susceptible to difference) to the inviolable identity of a monadic subject that serves as its own contingency.

Following the points of resemblance between the theological figure and Beckett's narrative trope, however, we must conclude that the dependency of the former on a miracle of transcendence reveals a crucial weakness of the latter. Like the Godhead, the first term of the theological figure, the first term or tenor of Beckett's causal trope—that is, the voice—can be granted causal status only as an absent cause, a kind of transcendental ego, a nonpositional consciousness, a being in itself. Because the master voice cannot be named or personified (it is not possessed of particular qualities), the causal efficacy of the master's voice is registered only through its effects, which hence serve the function of a substitutional term. Consequently, the full articulation of this causality must defer to the very multiplicity (or heterogeneity and contradiction) that was the pretext of such elaborate figuration in the first place. We have posited resemblance only to return to difference. Cause (narrator as cause of Pim) becomes effect (narrator as narrated along with Pim, Krim, Kram, Bom) becomes cause (the revealed source of quotational speech). The rhetorical privileging of heterogeneous order over homogeneous order in this schema for *How It Is* establishes contradiction or discontinuity as a criterion of intelligibility. This is confirmed by the narrator's ultimate confession that Pim, the "master voice," and all the extrapolations of Bem, Bom, Krim, and Kram (metaphoric extensions of the essential structure of unifying relations) are a pure heuristic intended to appease the narrator's self-doubt. In this way, all the cause-inflicting "others" ultimately revert to the narrator. But we must not forget that identity in this case is contingent upon its own displacement. The ultimate contradiction becomes the ultimate negation. The narrator must deny everything but the voice of denial:

> never any procession [the movement towards Pim] no or
> any journey, no never any Pim no no Bom, no never anyone
> no only me no answer. (146)

Because this "only" narrator is posited within a field of limitless contradictions, he exists without the relational certainty of the causal trope he announces. Without such stability, subjectivity becomes nomadic.

As it turns out, the untranscendable present tense of Beckett's title, *How It Is*, proves prophetic of this narrator's inability to temporalize the narrative with a subject-inducing causality.

The concomitant absence of Aristotle's form-legitimating *telos* leads us to reconceive the category of the subject (the correlative of *telos* in any analysis of *mimesis*-creation) as an effect or ensemble of effects without a cause. The two-term relation whereby one code may be read in terms of another, such as the narrator-Pim *agon*, is denied its mediating status here by its displacement into a wider field of combinatory relations. This perhaps is Beckett's acknowledgment of the "mess" that art confronts in its formal rigor: "It [the mess] is all around us and our only chance now is to let it in. The only chance of renovation is to open our eyes and see the mess."[12] When Beckett insists that, properly speaking, literary form does not eliminate the mess, he posits a novel idea of literary practice. We can more astutely speculate how Beckett's way of inhabiting human subjectivity suggests an original understanding of literary practice if we recall Beckett's commitment to an authorial creation that admits of nothing to express. Such, we recall, was the art of the Dutch painter Bram Van Velde, whom Beckett applauds for "submit[ing] to the incoercible absence of terms." We may now say that the absence of terms is Beckett's explicit theme in *How It Is*, at least in the sense that the usual contrast between subjects and objects, causes and effects, is broken. The disparity between a literary form that carries an already articulated message along its discursive trajectory and one whose expressive potential is constituted in an original lack (articulated as difference) appears most sharply in Beckett's title.

Despite all of Beckett's somber teasing of the mystery of being (primordial presence) with the portentous declarative of his title, the "it" in *How It Is* speaks reflexively for itself, for the absence of other terms that it encodes with meaning or that decode its meaning. Indeed, I would like to generalize on this basis to say that the relational structure of subjectivity in *How It Is* is the sum of locutionary contingencies that articulate the text. That is why the book offers no easy subordination of parts to wholes but instead a concatenation of partial perspectives. My point becomes clearer in the observation that the position of the grammatical subject in Beckett's title is occupied by what linguists call a shifter.[13] The shifter is the linguistic unit that simply marks positionality of the subject as sender of the message without anchoring it in an order that transcends the locutionary. The shifter marks a syntactical threshold of the narrative, pointing us to a level of analysis where we can map the shifts of locutionary direction without deferring to categories of character or voice. These categories mire us in an epistemology already discredited by the formal organization of the work. And so it is at the locutionary level of the text that our study must continue.

III

To state my arguments thus far: in the narrative form of *How It Is*, Beckett gives us the play between two kinds of knowledge—a knowledge revealed by the reduction of differences and assimilable to the form of linear causality, will, expression, monadic subjectivity—and a knowledge proliferated in difference and apparently disunified, unwilled, and unexpressive. This dualism recalls the two registers of trope proposed in Ricoeur's study of metaphor. Ricoeur holds that the difference between a predicative or live metaphor and a denominative or dead metaphor is that with the predicative metaphor, change occurs at the level of the linguistic code and not of the individual word. The denominative or name-transference model of trope presupposes terms to which the substituted terms are automatically reducible. The predicative trope (more compatible with the vision of an artist like Bram Van Velde) presupposes an absence of terms, at least in the sense that the proper integration of the substituting term necessitates a retextualizing or rewriting of the predicate to which it applies. A substitution of one term for another is impossible because the ratio of resemblance to difference is not stable. The contradictions that articulate the narrating subject of *How It Is* as an "absent cause" draw our attention away from the objects of predication—that

is, the claims of the narrator—to the contingencies of predication, the conditions of possibility that those claims invoke.

Because the predications of live metaphor are no longer unified by a coded homogeneity (and so we shift our emphasis to
the contingencies), they are subject to retextualization or reap-
propriation along a multiplicity of syntactical axes. On the most
elemental formal level of analysis applicable to Beckett's novel,
this shift of emphasis from form to contingencies of form is rendered grammatically. There are no clearly punctuated full predications in Beckett's novel. On the contrary, the tripartite arrangement of narrative elements (time before, time during,
and time after) is subdivided into strophic prose paragraphs
that, disjoined from one another, display internal syntactical
elisions. We must look at a full page of this prose for a perspective that reveals the impossibility of designating the subject in
familiar terms.

mine what I need that's it most need changing aspects
that's it ever changing aspects of the never changing life
according to the needs but the needs the needs surely for
ever here the same needs from age to age the same thirsts
the voice says so

it said I murmur for us here one after another the same
thirsts and life unchanging here as above according to the
unchanging needs hard to believe it depends on the moment the mood of the moment the mood remains a little
changeful you may say no sound there is nothing to prevent
you today I am perhaps not quite so sad as yesterday there
is nothing to stop you

the things I could no longer see little scenes part one in
their stead Pim's voice Pim in the light blue of day and blue
of night little scenes the curtains parted the mud parted
the light went on he saw for me that too may be said there
is nothing against it

silence more and more longer and longer silences vast
tracks of time we at a loss more and more he for answers I
for questions sick of life in the light one question how often
no more figures no more time vast figure vast stretch of
time on his life in the dark the mud before me mainly curiosity was he still alive YOUR LIFE HERE BEFORE ME
utter confusion (73)

Let us begin with a basic unit of this composition. More than
any other fragment on this page, "it said I" (in the second
strophe) sharply articulates Beckett's concern with the slippages between subject and object. In the objective case, "it,"
referring to the master's voice, fulfills the subject function here
while the object is designated by the subjective case. Yet by
the same token of grammatical regularity, we could choose to
respect the case priorities instead of the conventional syntactical priorities and insist upon a syntactical construal whereby
the "I" claims its status as agent. Or perhaps we have spliced
the locution incorrectly. Perhaps we have two statements: "It
said. I murmur." These constructions depend upon distinct
temporal or causal priorities.

Ordinarily we would choose the "correct" reading depending
on context: representational identity is confirmed by mutually
reinforcing predicates or by a set of discursive objects linked to
the same structure of intentionality. Husserlian phenomenology tells us that the subject is always *the subject of a predication*. The intentional consciousness constitutes itself in the
predication of objects, the thesis of being and ego both. Hence
we must look for a standard by which to judge the compatibility
of separate discursive objects in the text so that they reduce to
the same order of predication.

For Husserl, whom David Hesla cites as a thinker cognate
with Beckett's own epistemological predisposition, linguistic
reason is a concrete realization of the premise that the sign
is always constituted in the act of expressing meaning by a

speaker making a judgment on something.[14] Because the trappings of linguistic reason linking subject and object are lacking in Beckett's prose, we are tempted to put the text under the sign of an *aporia*, the ultimate absurdity.

And yet we cannot be convinced that this writing voids sense. After all, the words group themselves, idiomatically, into plausible statements even without the grammatical markers of punctuation. Yet the lack of punctuation allows contradictory construals such as I have described, which may be designated more precisely as syntactical antinomies. They present a formidable obstacle to sense, offering a conflicted context without supplying any way of resolving the conflict. In the face of these antinomies, proper grammatical construal must be deferred in favor of constructing the possible pretexts upon which it would depend. Without punctuation, the text demands that we acknowledge a field of semantic conditions of possibility wider than any one particular construal of meaning. And thus we are reminded that every construal of the conditions of possibility is itself a reconstruction of the "given" materials of a text that would have to be acknowledged. Before we consider "it said I" or "it said, I murmur," thus placing the objects of predication within a stable field of syntactical priorities, we must first improvise the coordinates of that field. Despite the phenomenological cast of this line of argument, our understanding of improvisation here precludes a unified intentional consciousness, a Husserlian idealism. Rather, it denotes the multiplication of perspectives determined in contradiction. By allowing diverse syntactical combination, Beckett's text produces a virtual reflexivity or a reflexivity without a subject to reflect. In other words, the text construes subjective reflexivity as a dynamic disjuncture. Reflexivity is the potential for rewriting inscribed in the overdeterminations of this text's unmarked syntax.

The remaining content of the paragraph we are discussing sheds some light on this hypothesis. Beckett's narrator announces that "the mood of the moment" is a determinant perspective of narrative. But we already know this to be an unacceptable concession to the fragmenting effect of time. The mood of the moment is the rising tide of successive moments eroding the structure of intentionality that this narrator has elaborately structured as causal propriety. In narratological theory, mood or point of view is a crucial mediator of narrative sense because it fixes the objects of a text within patterns of mutually supporting predications. But mood, as it is formulated in the work of Gérard Genette, is always dependent on a prior distinction between voice and speaker. Genette designates the speaker as the point of view expressed, whereas voice is marked in the particular locutions of textual utterance.[15] According to this analysis, the predications of a narrator are intelligible as they fit a binary opposition, the terms of which must be precisely stated.

It would be possible to elucidate Beckett's text by this means of analysis if we could distinguish Pim's speech in the quoted passage from the voice of the narrator. But if we were stymied in our efforts to parse "it said I," we will be even more discouraged by the narrator's subsequent disquisition on mood. Indeed, the "mood of the moment remains a little changeful" specifically by virtue of the narrator's subtle ventriloquism. We can't tell who is speaking. The concession to second-person singular "you may say so" would seem to offer the sought-after elucidation of point of view. But lacking a clear antecedent, the pronoun blurs instead of focuses. "You may say" collapses into "I am perhaps not quite so sad as yesterday," as if one point of view were rendered in two voices. As we saw when we tried to sort out the narrator's relation to Pim and the master voice, the narrator's self-deluding linear temporality depends upon the fiction of Pim's difference. Pim's autonomy (in this causal scheme) gives the narrator's appropriation of Pim dramatic significance just as the thesis of predication legitimates the operating consciousness of the transcendental ego. While the shift from "you" to "I" appears to structure the same difference between the narrator and Pim and thus establish a ratio of signification, the absence of a clear structure of antecedence nullifies the distinction and suggests a difference between narrator and Pim that remains a prior authenticating term of complementarity. The absence of punctuation vitiates the binary polarity of voice and speaker from which the notion of mood derives its significance. For this reason, we might say that the difference appearing in contradictions (at the level of voice) locks the text at the locutionary threshold. For that reason, mood is rendered an obsolete term for analysis of point of view. Point of view, then, is understood as a locus of contradiction.

This is, of course, another way of saying that Beckett calculates the impotence of conventional point of view as a potent narrative device. The phrase with which the narrator reflects this failure is "ever changing aspects of never changing life." This phrase concedes differential play of moments as a way of predicating the diversity of human experience with respect to the identity of human consciousness. Life is a need articulated by difference. This formulation of difference and identity is an illuminating structure of reflexivity for the narrator. Whereas the priority of life as a determinate signified is assumed by the narrator, the lack of any such fixed determination is affirmed by his syntax. Paradoxically, this rhetorical density hints at a narrative project that seems intended as a flight from the self rather than a reification of the self-representational I. Instead of elucidating the self-representational project of narrative through mood, Beckett elaborates internal contradictions as they in turn reveal new contingencies of predication. These are the antinomies of syntactical improvisation confronting the reader. They deploy the contradictions as transitions to new combinations. In this way the position of the subject, such as it is, is coextensive with the whole network of contingencies illuminated and sustained in contradiction.

I want to emphasize how fluent this description of the text would be with Beckett's own concept of creative act resisting the "sanity of a cause." The particular value of this text might be that it gives us a form that can sustain Beckett's theoretical project in the *Proust* monograph and the interview with Tom Driver. For his text is a form that "exists as a problem separate from the material it accommodates." The text never relapses into a comfortable presentation of first-person subjectivity or even a complex ironic subjectivity aware/unaware of its self-serving duplicates (such as the narrator ventriloquizing Pim). Rather, the syntactical heterogeneity within which this subjectivity appears is preserved as a condition of the subjectivity's possibility. I am not saying that Beckett's apparently syntaxless, unpunctuated prose nullifies predicative meaning. Rather, it puts such meaning in a dynamic relation with the chaos it nominally stands against.

The final strophe of the quoted page decisively punctuates the narrator's desire for a response, as he awaits Pim's recitation of life before this time with the narrator. In Pim's narration, the narrator seeks a term with which he could fashion some informing complementarity out of his own narrative stance, a beginning for which he can supply an end, a vehicle for which he can postulate a tenor, an effect for his cause. Yet all the narrator elicits are the words "utter confusion." These last words on the page issue a characteristic multiplicity of messages. The words may be read simply as the ventriloquized Pim's confession that life before the narrator was a state of confusion. Or the phrase may self-consciously display the narrator's confession that without a response from Pim his own unanswered question isolates him in confusion. Or the phrase may be a directive informed by the knowledge that to express oneself at all is to utter confusion. Indeed, the very ambiguity of the phrase bears out the fatalism of such a directive: to speak is to utter confusion. The impulse to speech is the never-changing need to which the ever-changing aspects of this narrative allude. It is precisely this need that the narrative cannot name or assign qualities to except in the disjunctures it presents. The inevitable confusion to which speaking consciousness returns may not, however, simply nullify sense-making possibilities of speech. On the contrary, it may guarantee the possibility that speech can continue through reconstructive possibilities of language disclosed only in the fertile rifts of syntactical displacements. Beckett's refusal to justify the ambiguity of utter confusion against a contextual norm (that is, to resolve its confusion) suggests that for him confusion is a kind of lucidity that relates fundamentally to the situation of the speaking subject in his time of narrative need. The surface confusion of Beckett's language in such moments at least prompts us to recall that confusion has always been an identifying trait of poetic language. It speaks implicitly for an expressive need we can acknowledge only at the limits of the available expressive forms of language—the preserve of the avant-garde with which Beckett's name has always been synonymous.

IV

Among theorists who have sought to account for the distinguishing features of avant-garde discourses and the confusions that attend them, Julia Kristeva is one of the most articulate. Kristeva, educated in the foundations of Lacanian psychoanalysis, distinguishes the symbolic function (language as nomination, sign, and syntax), the naming-predicative function, from the semiotic, nonthetic mode of signification. The concept of the semiotic relates the category of the subject to the body of instinctual drives, "a heterogeneousness to meaning and signification," which, like the Freudian unconscious, "shapes the signifying function" and hence is the counter of poetic language:

> the thetic predicative operation and its correlates (signified object and transcendental ego) though valid for the signifying economy of poetic language are only one of its *limits* [my emphasis]. . . . While poetic language can indeed be studied through its meaning and signification (by revealing depending on method either structure or process) such a study would in the final analysis amount to reducing it to the phenomenological perspective and hence failing to see

what in the poetic function departs from the signified and the transcendental ego and makes of what is known as "literature" something other than knowledge; the very place where the social code is destroyed and renewed.[16]

In this analysis, Kristeva situates literary language within Lacan's dialectic of desire. As we saw in chapter three, for Lacan the acquisition of language is an extremity of the Oedipal complex wherein the child compensates for the unreliability of the mother's presence by inserting him- or herself into the signifying order of social codes.[17] In this way, the child restores personal integrity, somatic wholeness having been lost upon the removal of the mother's body. The child's need for the mother's love (body) is postulated as an absent cause insofar as the child's power of signification arises in the place of an other, that is, language as social code. The shattering difference that divides the child from him- or herself when the mother departs compels the child to find a surrogate gratification. But because the need satisfied by the mother's presence is universal (it is the unconditionality of the child's need for love), the child's entrance into the chain of signifiers in the place of the (m)other leaves "a metonymic residue which runs under the chain of signifiers, an indeterminate element which is at once absolute but untenable . . . called desire."[18] Lacan's own elucidation of this residue strikingly recalls the narrator's relation to Pim in *How It Is*: soliciting speech, song, silence, satisfying himself in a succession of utterances that never restore a sense of wholeness or completeness or—what is more important—temporal unity. For, in the Lacanian scheme, when the child's demand for unconditional love (the mother's body) is articulated for the satisfaction of a single need (such as food), the specific reason for demand is removed but the coexistent totality of needs remains unsatisfied and hence unrepresented, producing a sense of loss and thus impelling the further production of signs. The production of signs in desire is a calculable ratio with loss. Kristeva gives us a rhetorical grasp of the "constitutive" loss inherent in signification or production of literature in her definition of semiotic discursiveness. The semiotic for her is "a distinctiveness admitting of an uncertain and indeterminate articulation because it does not yet refer . . . to a signified object for a thetic consciousness."[19] The semiotic runs counter to literature inasmuch as it belies the sufficiency of symbolic language to an individual subjective intent, defying the automatic closure of full predication. I believe Beckett's phrase "ever changing aspects of a never changing life" (later "life" becomes "need") eloquently grasps the paradox of his own narrative practice. The phrase alleges the inexpressibility of the need for meaning except by a radical divestiture of meaning. For while it stands as a bulwark against the atomization of the narrator's temporal experience, the phrase collapses logically for the reader under its imputation of a causality ("never changing need") that has no content, except retrospectively—at least insofar as contradictory aspects make cause construable from a diverse range of contingencies. But as Lacan says, "there is no such thing as a cause unless there is something amiss."[20] Literature decisively puts things amiss in the play of the semiotic and the symbolic. *How It Is* comprehensively articulates this play for the reader in the ready scannability of Beckett's prose on the one hand and the unscannable, unpunctuated syntactical mobility of the text on the other. The resultant confusion in Beckett's prose presents a dialectic between the apparent predications that fix the place of subjective intention and the real syntactical antinomies ("something amiss") that, through ambiguous contextual contiguities, restructure patterns of association.

I have placed Beckett's style here in the context of Kristeva's and Lacan's speculations because for all three the subject's access to language denotes a crisis in the subject of discourse. Supplying a useful framework for Beckett's own antiexpressive esthetic, Kristeva explains how it can be meaningful to discuss the absence of the subject in a literary form that undeniably speaks in human voice. In literary language, the speaking subject is an unavoidable pretext of grammatical form, but she

stipulates that "it is nonetheless evident that this subject in order to ally with its heterogeneity must be, let us say, a ques-
tionable subject-in-process. It is of course Freud's theory of the
unconscious that allows the apprehension of such a subject."[21] I
will adopt this notion of a subject-in-process to speak about the
desire for meaning (which Beckett's narrator enacts and which
the text undercuts in the reader's mind) and the possibility
raised earlier that the "utter confusion" is related to the constitutive desires of subjective consciousness assumed in the
function of a narrator.

Just as the metonymic residue of desire issues in the production of signs in Lacanian theory, so the lack of syntactically
marked predications in *How It Is* determines new relations by
contiguity. These relations of contiguity semantically exceed
the grammatical signifieds that would be determined by less
ambiguous punctuation. Such excess thwarts the causal logic
whereby we assimilate objects to predicating subjects or vehi-
cles to tenors. The mechanism of this thwarting has been de-
lineated in Nietzsche's argument that causality is a trope: the
figure metonymy. I have been arguing that the causality of
Beckett's syntax is troped by a metonymic displacement. By
following the determinations of this displacement, we can map
the progress of the subject-in-process in Beckett's prose. Perhaps by this means we may make Kristeva's terms for the subject compatible with the metaphoric perspective I adopted earlier in this chapter as crucial to an understanding of Beckett's
subject.

One way of specifying the relevance of Beckett's narrative
practice for a theory of the subject is to observe that the preeminence of the metonymic axis in this discourse lends itself to
a much needed elucidation of the Lacanian Real. The Real is the
one cardinal concept of Lacanian epistemology that has not
been successfully bred with the terms of literary analysis, perhaps because it has too often been confused with a problematic
notion of the referent: reference as the postulate of an appropriate "outside" of discourse toward which the word is neces-

sarily solicitous. By contrast, the category of the Real is meaningful in psychoanalytical theories of narrative representation
as a heuristic. The Real is the unspecifiable ground term, the
absent cause that actualizes the interchange of sense and nonsense in narrative discourse. In strict psychoanalytical terms,
the Real, as that element of discourse "which resists symboliza-
tion absolutely,"[22] enables the succession of Oedipal consciousness and the passage of the subject from the imaginary to the
symbolic. As we have seen, the Oedipal stage occurs as the result of the interposition of a "third term" (the name-of-the-
father) into the circuits of the child-mother communication. The
child's unrationalized desire for meaning (the illusory self-
presence of Lacan's *imaginary* stage of consciousness) yields to
a complex substitutional logic (what Lacan calls the *symbolic*
stage). The insufficiency of every signifier to the inciting desire
(for presence) guarantees a metonymic concatenation of substitutive terms that propel the speaking subject into cultural
life. According to Lacan, this dynamic is expressed historically
in the social relations of power. The source of meaning (the un-
locatable referent), however, remains an endlessly deferred
question. In fact, the identity of the subject is constituted in
this deferral.

Similarly, in Beckett's prose, the elision of the predicative
place-of-the-subject poses a question about the source of meaning in narrative. Or we could say that the apparent syntactical
indeterminacy of Beckett's prose suggests that we need a new
theory of the subject, if we are to construe the narration as
something more than aimless discursive drift. The syntactical
overdetermination of semantic categories—that is, the constitutive power of sheer contiguity in Beckett's prose (in lieu of
the grammatical-semantic hierarchy of marked predicates)—
seems to foreclose on the category of the referent (univocality
or the mirror phase), unless of course we reformulate our understanding of the referent. Fredric Jameson's advocacy of
what he calls a materialist philosophy stands upon the proposition that any discussion of the referent must, in light of Lacan,

be severed from the realm of the signified and hence from the notion of a static subject:

> The chief defect of all hitherto existing materialism is that it has been conceived as a series of propositions about matter—and in particular the relationship of matter to consciousness, which is to say of the natural sciences to the so-called human sciences—rather than as a set of propositions about language. A materialistic philosophy of language is not a semanticism, naive or otherwise, because its fundamental tenet is a rigorous distinction between the signified—the realm of semantics proper, of interpretation, of the study of the text's ostensible meaning—and the referent. The study of the referent, however, is the study not of the meaning of the text, but of the limits of its meanings and of their historical preconditions, and of *what is and must remain incommensurable with individual expression* [my emphasis].[23]

Beckett is implicated in the claims of a materialistic esthetic insofar as the metonymic displacement of univocal (metaphoric) predications that distinguishes his prose style exhibits conditions of possibility rather than objectifiable "truths" of discourse. Point of view remains "incommensurable with individual expression" or univocal predication. Beckett's unmarked syntax, or the prevailing principle of contiguity in his prose, is, like the Lacanian "third term" (the Real), what makes the shift from an imaginary to a symbolic discourse conceptually possible. In other words, discontinuity is structurally significant here because it makes the limits of meaning, not meaning itself, the epistemological burden of the text. We could transpose this argument into the terms of my earlier discussion of predicative trope and say that denominative metaphor, which depends on marked predication (where terms are substitutable because they have fixed places), is functionally equivalent to the imaginary register of discourse. Correspondingly, the catachrestic or metonymic distribution of the denominative "place-of-the-subject" in Beckett's unmarked syntax is consistent with the symbolic register: the transition from one mode to the other signifies the Real, now viably conceived as a subject-in-process or a variable subjective positionality (*atopia*). This analysis then gives us a way of understanding the formidable constraints that are placed upon narrative will within the context of the anti-idealist, materialist epistemology presupposed in Beckett's text.

The most explicit dramatization of these constraints in *How It Is* appears in the lines immediately preceding the passage I last considered. The narrator's desire to represent himself summons the realization that his life is caught up in a mechanical cycle of repetitions:

> dear Pim come back from the living he got it from another
> that dog's life to take and to leave I'll give it to another the
> voice said so the voice in me that was without quaqua (72–73)

Though there may be multiple voices here, the passage suggests that there is only one story to tell, one meaning prior to existence to which all existents owe a narrative debt. The sentence glosses the epistemological predicament of the narrator, who, bound by the convention to tell this story, naively traps himself in a fatal self-repetition. The repetition is fatal because it blocks access to the place of an "other" that would otherwise be sought (in the dialogical response of a real, not a ventriloquized, Pim) as the ground of communication, the legitimate theater of this desire. Indeed, the narrator's devoutly wished-for end—"After Part Three, after Pim"—posits the goal of a moment decisively situated outside the tedious cycle of repetitions. Such a moment would by definition be lacking to the thetic consciousness of the narrator in the predicative slippages of this narration.

As I have been suggesting, this slippage posits an alternative mode of self-representation. In fact, the play between symbolic and semiotic (which I have alleged makes such an alternative possible) is revealed by a strategy of explicit locutionary repetitions in Beckett's prose. While these repetitions do not coalesce semantically, they foster contextual permutation. The phrases "brief movements of the lower face," indicating speech in the mud, and "vast tracts of time," denoting the uninterrupted temporal continuum that reduces all difference to sameness, sound a conspicuous refrain pertinent to the act of narrative. The narrator is moving his mouth in endless repetition of silent vocables. Like the "movements of the lower face," patterns of repetition in Beckett's prose collect no reservoirs of semantic sense. They only clear syntactical space. Thus the contextual permutations produced by repetition are more articulate than the fixed subjective positionality they seem to denote.

The most illuminating example of the discursive flexibility that Beckett achieves with this technique appears in his deployment of visual imagery. The fixed image typically indicates the stability of point of view within which the predicative strategies of more conventional narratives are determined. In *How It Is*, however, the fate of the image is linked to a proliferation of predicative possibilities. Toward the conclusion of Part One, which is the first term of the tripartite relational structure invoking the principles of an irresistible closure, the narrator dreams a peculiarly unclosed dream. The dream convention, evoking a dyadic conscious state, suggests the relevance of the relational dyads, literal and metaphorical, cause and effect. We might therefore expect the imagistic content of the dream to stand in a relation of logical priority with its contextual terms. A clue to the true relational meaning of the dream, however, appears in the transitional passage before the dream, a sophistic quibble about the priority of words and "movements of the lower face": "its my words come first then its they cause my words its one or the other I'll fall asleep within humanity again just barely." Cause and effect will have meaning now according to the interchange of sense and nonsense. Despite its apparent visual clarity, the imagery of the dream is "asleep" to the dictates of causal determination, as we can see if we examine the passage. The organizational mode of the passage is repetition, but the disposition of details within the pattern of repetition does not serve as a controlling first term to which all else can be referred in order to mirror its sense.

> the dust there was then the mingled lime and granite stones piled up to make a wall further on the thorn in flower green and white quickset mingled privet and thorn

> the depth of dust there was then the little feet big for their age bare in the dust

> the satchel under the arse the back against the wall raise the eyes to the blue wake up in a sweat the white there was then the little clouds you could see the blue through the hot stones through the jersey striped horizontally blue and white

> raise the eyes look for faces in the sky animals in the sky fall asleep and there a beautiful youth meet a beautiful youth with golden goatee clad in an alb wake up in a sweat and have met Jesus in a dream (45)

The imagery of this dream shimmers as a reflection on a watery surface: a lucidity always on the verge of dissolution. The dust—the proper medium for a literal "mingling" of lime and granite—is dislocated to a metaphorical contextual logic by the syntactical subordination of "mingled" to whole "stones." The syntactical tension of the passage is further complicated by the contextual pull of the verb "piled." Further on, the metaphoric contextual construal of "mingled lime and granite" would be literalized by the verb "piled" with "stones" would support this construal. Contextual contiguity here functions to revise literal-figurative priorities much as an unexpected effect relates to a hypostatic cause. If we recall the initial confusion of cause and effect—does the mouth cause the words or vice versa—at the beginning of the passage, we can see that Beckett's concern here is with the displacement from one causal pattern to another, and the interrelations spawned thereby.

In the second strophe, the repeated phrase "the depth of dust there was" establishes an ostensible continuity with the mingled lime and granite. But the phrase "little feet big for their age" does not fill out the prior scene; rather, it determines new contextual coordinates. The scene denoted in the first image of the dream is not reasserted out of the confluence of descriptive particulars but is redeployed so that the deep dust operates contextually not as a cause (as we might infer from the idea of people walking in the deep dust—dust as the medium of footprints is an efficient cause) but as an effect of "little feet big for their age, bare in the dust." It is an effect to the extent that the contextual logic organized by bare feet does not refer the image to the scenic or categorical anteriority of dust but rather articulates an a postiori contingency. It is as ambiguous and exemplary a sign as a real footprint in the sand. The footprint, like any rhetorical figure, is alternately an index of the ground by virtue of its depth and a sign raising the ground to consciousness in the contours of its figural relief. What is suggested is the potential reciprocity between literal and metaphorical meaning.

Furthermore, the visual resolution of the dream imagery in this passage dissolves under the pressure of conflicting perspectives, much as we have seen thetic predication dissolve in the free solution of unpunctuated grammatical elements. For example, the "satchel," "arse," and "wall"—evocations of the body of the dreamer—denote a visual point of view that quickly transforms the object that determined it. The vision of white clouds through which the blue can be seen, the hot stones (presumably of the wall), and the jersey (presumably clothing the body) do not come into focus as integrated elements of a scene determined by a unique perspectival horizon. Such a horizon would structure relations of resemblance or semantic complementarity—equalities of one thing with another—much as denominative metaphor does. But here syntactical contiguities overshadow the semantic continuities by revealing new combinatory possibilities that are not recursive. "The white there was then," while seeming to echo the idiom of the earlier "the dust there was," nonetheless isolates the noun "white" without any connection to the previous noun, "dust." The resulting abstraction is quickly appeased by the metaphoric assimilation of white to clouds, which radically alters the scenic potential. The white is causally reduced in a manner suggestive of denotative metaphor or synecdoche. But once again the immanent value of the image is quickly diminished by the ungoverned syntactical concatenation of "you could see the blue through," turning the causal cloud into a contingency of the view of the sky. The field of combinatory possibilities is further complicated by the syntactical antimony of "through the hot stones," assuming the preposition is construed to link "you" to "hot stones" rather than to "clouds" or to both. The repetition of the prepositional link "through" concatenates a syntactical possibility that further displaces the subject. The color of clothing mirroring the blue and white of the sky suggests both a metaphoric likeness and a paradoxical scenic dissociation. The only continuity is the continuity of transition from one predicative vantage point to another. The shifting positionality of the predicating subject is registered as the reassignment of ostensible effects as causes. Just as the clouds are both objects of perceptions and mediations of second-order perceptions, the hot stones are both objectified by the preposition "through" and dislocated from the predication by its slippage to the position of subject or cause of vision through the jersey. In the contrast between seeing through clouds and seeing through stones/clothes, we are reminded that logical "sense," like the punning dimension harbored in the word *sense*'s being physical and mental, always juxtaposes a dispersive heterogeneity with the reductive teleology of linear logic.

The locutionary ambiguity of the dream brings this out most emphatically in its conclusion. The dreamer's apotheosis is "met a beautiful youth with golden goatee clad in an alb wake up in a sweat and have met Jesus in a dream." Here with almost parodic punctuality is the teleological purpose par excellence: on the one hand, an effect disguised as a cause (as if all the elements of the dream could be unified in the name Jesus, just as the son of God becomes the cause of man's salvation), but on the other hand, an effect devoid of the structure of contextual resemblances that makes such an outcome plausible in narrative terms. Because the imagistic incarnation of Jesus is not coherent with the other imagistic particulars of the dream, the name functions without this context much as God does—that is, by transcendence. The resolution of the dream is such that the name Jesus serves as a tenor to which the disjunctive particulars of the dream are assimilable by virtue of a prior conceptual identity: Christ and the sins of man. But just as the transcendent logic of Beckett's tripartite plot structure (positing an identity) collapses into difference, so the name Jesus functions rhetorically as a contingency to which the previous imagistic particulars are assimilable only as they are in turn subject to an exogenous dispersive causality. In other words, the dream offers a unique form of knowledge, specifically, in the words of Beckett's narrator, "that kind of image not for the eyes not for the ears" (45). An image, insofar as it cites an object for predications, functions like a name, for example, Jesus. But the kind of image the narrator "speaks" here is preeminently for the mind, or of the mind. Perhaps we can say that the distinction is that it serves a constitutive, not an imitative, function. Like all the rhetorical tropes that expose the hidden contingencies of proper names, this "image" depends on an apparent arbitrariness for which already acknowledged causes such as a visible object are not sufficient. That is, this image, like a challenging metaphor, entails an apparent arbitrariness insofar as it deconstructs the perspective that invoked it.

For an elegant account of the constitutive arbitrariness of creative acts, consider Kenneth Burke's coinage of the term "deflection." Unlike the more programmatic deconstructionist

critics whose legitimation of arbitrariness (by way of Saus-
surean sanction) denies determinate motivational grounds,
Burke avoids the regress of radical indeterminacy. Burke argues that deflection—"any slight bias or unintended error"—is
the rhetorical basis of all language and determinate meaning,
"a dialectical subversion of the consistent link between sign
and meaning in grammatical patterns."[24] In A Grammar of
Motives, Burke more explicitly links arbitrariness with the creative act. He affirms that the creative artist must seek a locus
of motives within action (creation) itself if he or she is to avoid
the trap of pantheistic philosophies that seek to posit an immanent creation (where act collapses into agent). Every true act
of creation denotes "a newness not already present" in the
terms of its articulation.[25] God's will is not his creation if it is
conterminous with his nature. On the contrary, effective creation bears the mark of a fertile discontinuity. Fritz Mauthner,
one of Beckett's candidly acknowledged intellectual sources and
the author of a polemical treatise attempting to pierce the pretension of language to grasp a world of being, offers a version of
Burke that links Beckett to these ideas.

Mauthner cites the ambiguity of the German word Zufall-
sinne (accidental or chance occurrence of senses) to argue that
the basis of linguistic invention and hence conceptual mobility
is the inevitable slippage between sameness and similarity
from which memory professes to protect us:

> without this essential mistake there would not be a devel-
> opment in the organic world and in the world of the mind
> there would not be any concepts or words.[26]

What Burke and Mauthner understand about the traps of a
language whose predications revert to unifying structures of
resemblance Beckett also understands very well. Beckett's insight is focused in his exposition of Proust's "involuntary memory." Involuntary memory's activity of unsolicited resemblance
affords the possibility of authentic action in a Burkeian sense

because it cancels the "countless treaties concluded between the countless subjects that constitute the individual and the countless correlative objects." Proustian memory—because it is simultaneously "an evocation and a direct perception, because it is its own contingency—displays the conditions of its own possibility rather than the essence of the past. It is what Beckett designates as the "ideal real."[27] It is both imaginative and empirical, a relation of particulars determined by the network of contingencies they articulate (rather than a relation determined in contingencies). To recast this discussion in terms of self and other, we can say that an expression of the continuity of the self based on a unified ego depends on already presented terms. The narrating self in *How It Is* speaks for the absence of such terms.

When Beckett insists upon acknowledgment of the "absence of terms" as the condition of artistic creation while also insisting on the formal integrity of the creation, he suggests a model of causality that strains our familiar view of the world. For this reason, I will not hesitate to look beyond familiar contexts for an aid to the exposition of these ideas. The Marxist philosopher Louis Althusser, in a quest that is only topically unrelated to Beckett's project, seeks an explanation of how we can "think the effectivity of a structural system on its elements"[28] without becoming metaphysical. A relation exists between political economy, which is Althusser's subject, and the economy of the subject, which, I argue, Beckett's rhetorical strategies elucidate. Just as the structure of Beckett's narrative demands a notion of causality that does not reduce to an inner essence, a self, a subject, Althusser argues that to study the structure constituting and determining economic objects demands that the production of the concept of that object be the absolute condition of its theoretical possibility. Althusser conceives the necessity of a "structural causality" displaying the "mode of presence of the structure of economic objects in its effects." Critical of the expressive and transitive models of causality dominant in Western epistemologies (they unify a system by postulating a complementary inside-outside), Althusser insists upon the hypothesis of an "absent cause." In this way he invalidates the categorical oppositions of essence and phenomenon that turn analysis toward metaphysics:

> The absence of the cause in the structure's metonymic causality on its effects is not the fault of the exteriority of the structure with respect to the economic phenomena; on the contrary, it is the very form of the interiority of the structure as a structure in its effects.[29]

Beckett's praise for the Proustian ideal real is consistent with Althusser's recognition that a linear causality will not elucidate a phenomenon determined by its own "complexity." "Complexity" here denotes the need to produce a concept of the object or the need to acknowledge the object by constructing the field in which it is discovered. For Beckett, the ideal real reveals this complexity because it annuls time. Hence it realizes the concreteness of the unique moment. In Beckett's view, time, like the tripartite structure of *How It Is*, is only a formula for identity, and that identity is death. Death, the tenor of the events of our life, does not lend itself to art because it posits "a unity abstract from plurality." If, as Beckett tells us in *Proust*, the ideal of the ideal real is the death of time, we are certain to recognize the proliferation of unassimilable contingencies in Beckett's prose as a product of the same idealism. Beckett gives us a plurality unified by the articulation of its own diversity. But we must not view Beckett's prose style in *How It Is* simply as an argument against closure, an invitation to indeterminacy.

Rather, the positive determinations of this prose style afford a powerful conceptualization of the narrating subject. The movement from the potentially full predication (locutionary repetitions, scannable syntax, etc.) to the actual syntactical dispersals that empty them can best be described, as I have said, in terms of the drift from metaphor to metonymy. I have said that this entails a reflexivity founded on contradiction or contiguity with a heterogeneous outside. It is reflexive insofar as the subject's conditions of possibility are both the terms of its articulation and the object to be constructed. In the wake of the dream passage discussed earlier, Beckett's narrator provisionally sums up the condition of his mind in a phrase that acutely reflects the actual progress of the narrative more than the belief—in ends—that is credited with motivating it. For he is "seeking that which I have lost there where I have never been" (47). We might say that in Beckett's style the subject looking for itself in a hypostatic effect paradoxically finds itself in the willful deflections from that end.

I have argued that the shaping figure of Beckett's prose in *How It Is* is metaphor insofar as the repetitions of the text, whether imagistic or idiomatic, appear to structure relations based on resemblance. But just as the need to establish ends and hence a pretext for resemblance is the motivating fiction of Beckett's narrator, the sustaining fiction of Beckett's narrative, I believe, is the knowledge that to pursue ends that have propped one's beginnings is only to indulge a morbid fascination. Even the narrator who sets out by establishing ends in order not to "die before his time" must proceed by denying death its privileged status as a solitary contingency. This is the motive for multiplying contingencies that deflect from the morbid closure of resemblance. The vitality of metaphoric logic in *How It Is* arises not out of the resolution of sameness in diversity but in the construal of diversity out of sameness. As Ricoeur implies, only by virtue of such a recasting of the relational density of metaphor can we conceive of a matrix within which metaphor generates change at the level of the linguistic code rather than at the level of the word.

The compatibility of Beckett's metaphoric style with Althusser's claims for a structural causality reveals Beckett's engagement with the problem of the subject to be one that seeks a profound revolution on the level of the code of cultural representations and not just on the level of dramatic *mise-en-scène*. If we take ideology to be, as Althusser says, "the imaginary representation of the subject's relationship to his or her real condition of existence,"[30] we can see that the mode of representation of the subject in *How It Is* has significant implications in a world of human actions. In ideology, the relations of representation for the subject are fixed with respect to a specific order of reality.[31] Because the subject in *How It Is* is not a hypostatic cause, not a fixed place of intelligibility (as Barthes describes the classical novel), it invites speculation that Kristeva's abstract formulation of a subject-in-process might find its desirable specifications in Beckett's text. The process of this subject-in-process is given exposition here as a network of contingencies rather than the dissolution of contingencies in a causal ratio. In Beckett, the meaning of the subject-in-process is articulated as a relation of difference produced within the alternation between metaphoric inclusiveness and metonymic exclusions. The absence of syntactical teleology guarantees an excess of signification.

This is amply illustrated at the end of Beckett's narrative, where the narrative voice in the throes of formal closure must take upon himself all the causes of his own effect. Reduced in this way to the circumstantial knowledge that he is his own ventriloquist's doll, but desiring still to control narrative developments, he has recourse only to the act of producing a difference within himself as the basis of that development. The tantalizing goal the narrator offers himself in the dream of closure seems at the "end" of this novel to retain vitality through a self-deception: a deferral of the act of closure in favor of the explanation of its conditions of possibility. He concludes:

> good good end at last of part three and last that's how it
> was end of quotation after Pim how it is (147)

Having moved from one position to another toward the relation of identity, the postulate of closure—"end of quotation"— the narrator finds himself only in another position with its own contingencies to disclose. There is no final position, nor, I would

argue, would we want there to be. Characteristically, the metaphoric gesture of thrusting the narrative into the past tense in
the last paragraph of the novel—"that's how it was end of
quotation after Pim"—instantly entails the contradictory, dispersive metonymic contingencies of the present ("how it is").

Subjectivity in Beckett's novel appears under the sign of the
present tense because the present is the preservation of a lack,
an equivalent to the place of the other. It is a kind of silence.
But I would say that the much-hallowed silences of Beckett's
art have been misunderstood by critics when perceived merely
as a reverence for the impassable threshold of consciousness.
Rather, this silence echoes the need of consciousness for elision
of its own thetic prowess. Ironically enough, this credo is nowhere more declamatory in Beckett's *oeuvre* than in *The Dream
of Fair to Middling Women*, his only completely unpublished,
unspoken work:

> The experience of my reader shall be between the phrases,
> in the silence, communicated by the intervals, not the terms
> of the statement, between the flowers that cannot coexist
> at the antithetical (nothing so simple as antithetical) sea-
> sons of words, his experience shall be the menace, the mir-
> acle, the memory, of an unspeakable trajectory.[32]

Certainly nothing so simple as the antithesis of speech and silence adequately accounts for the complexity of Beckett's fiction. Neither speech nor silence is an informative term within
the terms of their opposition. Or perhaps Beckett would say
they are too much terms of analysis, thereby precluding new
discursive positions for the subject. If silence is preeminent in
Beckett's work, it is so metaphorically insofar as the creative
act "voices" only the constraints upon its own expression. But
this is neither nihilism nor sentimental existentialism. This
"gapped discourse" insists upon the human need of expression
as a determinate exigency of human nature. Beckett will not
betray that nature by hypostatizing particular expressions—to

contrive such ends would be to abstract the vitally inconclusive duration of living. On the contrary, the last line in Beckett's narration, wavering on the threshold of contradiction, denotes the durance of need itself. The need of the present informs every act by which we seek to escape the tautological and deathly recognitions of the past.

6
NARRATIVE
AS
EVENT
AND
ACT

> The act of thinking does not proceed from a simple
> natural possibility; on the contrary, it is the only true
> creation. Creation is the genesis of the act of thinking
> within thought itself. This genesis implicates something
> which does violence to thought, which wrests it from its
> natural stupor, and its merely abstract possibilities.
>
> Gilles Deleuze,
> *Proust and Signs*

In its Aristotelian essentials—plot and character—the novel is conventionally a ratio of ends and means. The incremental events of narrative plot traditionally gain significance in commensuration with a resolving horizon of expectations. This is the "identity principle" of *dénouement* whereby apparent differences miraculously integrate new criteria of relatedness; conflict is appeased by revised parameters of inclusiveness. I have sought to examine narrative within a rhetorical perspective provided by metaphor because I detect a homologous relation between the causal, unifying logic of linear narrative and the conceptual synthesis performed by trope. Both are based on a principle of resemblance. Yet despite the spectacular domi-

nance of this form-giving rule of resemblances, novelists from
Sterne to Robbe-Grillet[1] have struggled to free themselves
from the patriarchal fatalism of its determinations. Subsist-
ing in shadows cast by the most imposing conventional forms
are their dialogical counterparts: novels that interrogate the
ground of their own formal unity.

Of course, to comprehend texts that self-consciously contest
the totalizing authority of linear plot, we must discover a calculus for the relationship of parts and wholes distinct from the
identity principle of *dénouement*. To this end, I have contrasted the gapped narrative of avant-garde texts with the orthodox teleology of closed plots by distinguishing between two
versions of metaphoric trope. I used the Renaissance term catachresis to distinguish a relational knowledge predicated on difference from the name-transference function of denominative
metaphor predicated on resemblance.

I found the cue for such analysis in the practice of writers
whose texts make discontinuity, rather than the thematic continuity of fate-identity, the criterion of knowledge and intelligibility. Discontinuity resists the totalizing predicates of linear plot. Of course, in the relativistic climate of contemporary
criticism, under the unrelenting light of deconstruction and
surfictionist reflexivities, any serious interpretive project is
virtually obliged to interrogate closed systems of representation. In this respect my choice of texts that fight against easy
closure must appear merely, if grudgingly, symptomatic of the
times. Nevertheless, I have chosen this focus and these texts
not to hypostatize a revolution of style in the novel or in criticism but rather to probe the presuppositions of typical practices
for a fuller account of the motivational springs of narrative.

Of course, mine is not an original or solitary endeavor. Any-
one who has followed the drift of contemporary theory will note
that the problems I have discussed here—the relation of character to plot, plot to *mimesis*, fate to identity—are all featured
in the currently popular narratological criticism. The narratological approach with its taxonomically privileged catego-

ries of Proppian functions or Greimasian *actants*, etc., seems perfectly fluent with the distinctive formal properties of avant-garde fiction presented by Djuna Barnes, John Hawkes, and Samuel Beckett.[2] Yet my own vocabulary and my preference for a rhetorical topos may appear willfully eccentric or woefully uninformed. Despite the fact that the rhetorical school holds sway over contemporary critical discourse in the names of de Man, Derrida, Kristeva, and others, it has tended more toward a general critique of culture than an analysis of genre. While narratology grows out of the structuralist seedbed, it has often preempted many of the theoretical perspectives offered by the rhetorical approach in the interest of genre specialization. I must therefore briefly try to place my own work with respect to the arguments of narratology, if only to show what objects are lost in the latter's narrowly converging lines of inquiry. My purpose, however, is not to open a full-scale debate in order to disprove the theoretical grounds of narratological dicta. I prefer to evoke a methodological contrast as a way of resolving a persistent theme of my own study: the need to make the transformations of contextual logic an important threshold of critical inquiry.

I began this book with the observation that a contradiction inevitably appears in the critical perspectives on modern and contemporary fiction. Critics find themselves torn between their desire to postulate a level of thematic unity in texts and their need to acknowledge an inherent discontinuity between the devices of thematic unity and the inherent duplicities of language. The appearance of this contradiction is perhaps symptomatic of a dualistic habit of thinking on which the narratological postulates subsist—a habit of mind that the experimental texts discussed here resist with all their formal rigor. This is my reason for seeking what I have at times called a materialist theory of narrative: where unity and difference are mutually articulate terms.

Narratologists propose to study the novel as a highly systematic reshuffling of binary choices. Narratology splits the

text into *fabula-sujet*, *histoire-recit*, or story-discourse, distinguishing the events of the story in their "real" temporality from
the order of their presentation. Seymour Chatman's recent
compendium of Russian and French schema, *Story and Discourse*, reveals that this methodological move (from which he
takes his title) involves us in some illuminating contradictions.
First, to conceive fable as a set of unmediated actions anterior
to plot (*mythos*) is to forget the temporal mediation by which
particulars can be construed as events in the first place. Chatman would distinguish *mythos* from event insofar as it denotes
the "arrangement" of events into sequences. He wants to preserve *mythos* as the place of invention, the locus of creative
agency. But if we remember that *fabula* is already "plotted"
temporally and that the temporal priority of this order gives it
a causal burden, Chatman's distinction may appear to undermine the very claims it is intended to serve. Chatman's distinction between fabula as "basic story stuff, the sum of total
events to be related in the narrative" and the "story as actually
told by linking the events together"[3] (this is really Victor
Erlich's exposition in *Russian Formalism: History and Doctrine*) implies that the constructive aspect of the text is always
disclosed as a second-order referent. This seems perversely
akin to a reflection theory of *mimesis* that privileges a world of
objects over a world of verbal determinations. To suggest an
original "story stuff" seems to reintroduce into an otherwise
vigilant and skeptical critical milieu a naive dualism such as
Paul Ricoeur detects in the canonical readings of Aristotle.[4] For
Ricoeur, remember, we are predisposed—according to our bias
for a reflection/copy theory of imitation—to separate *mythos*
from *mimesis* as though *mythos* were the order of events and
mimesis were the author's act of arranging them. On that
basis, we would privilege an essential temporal order. But privileging story over discourse where story is *mythos* and discourse is *mimesis* is of course precisely the opposite of what
narratologists like Chatman intend. Nevertheless, such a

strictly dualistic enterprise is eminently susceptible to just such confusions and tends to obscure a full account of the contextual determinations of narrative. Jonathan Culler suggests what is wrong with that analysis when he says:

> For the study of point of view to make sense there must be various contrasting ways of viewing and telling a given story, and this makes "story" an invariant core, a constant against which the variables of narrative presentation can be measured. But to describe the situation in this way is to identify the distinction as a heuristic fiction, for except in rare cases, the analyst is not presented with contrasting narratives of the same sequence of actions; the analyst is confronted with a single narrative and must postulate what "actually happens" in order to be able to describe and interpret the way in which this sequence of events is organized, evaluated and presented by the narrator.[5]

If we must discover the meaning of a narrative as variations of an invariant core, we have indeed established a context of understanding in which the creative act that Aristotle calls *mimesis* is superseded by a primary plotted temporal order— that is, *mythos*. Ricoeur insists that *mimesis* is production and grounded in *lexis*.[6] In this way, he unites *mimesis* with metaphor, the exemplary *lexis*. The narratological dichotomy of story and discourse, however, suggests a causal link between event and the sundry combinations to which it is susceptible. This analysis seems therefore to construe *mimesis* as reproduction instead of production. The necessary adequation of one code to another is identifiable with the model of denominative trope in which a strange term substituted for a familiar term precludes the possibility of significant invention by privileging a mediating resemblance. When confronted with this familiar account of the mediations of one code by another, one can easily object, along with critics like Frederic Jameson[7] (whose goals are ostensibly remote from mine but whose assumptions are not), that such transcodings promote a virtually tautological interpretation.

In this book, I have read texts that problematize the paradigms of narrative causality through a catachrestic rhetorical density. This is perhaps most acutely perceived in Beckett, where the understanding of metaphor is strained by the recognition of an inevitable slide into metonymy. The usual distinction between metaphor as a phenomenon of paradigmatic substitution and metonymy as a phenomenon of contextual contiguity is blurred by the writers discussed here through formal strategies that not only reverse the systematic reduction of resemblances but also proliferate material differences. The complementarity of literal and figurative codes can no longer be a controlling assumption of interpretation. Umberto Eco gives some critical leverage to writers like Beckett who are striving to overcome the metaphor-metonymy dualism through means that may appear (particularly to hostile critics) mere stylistic excess. In *The Response of the Reader*, Eco suggests that metaphorical intelligibility is necessarily contingent on the phenomenon of contiguity rather than a conceptual calculus prior to the linguistic matrix. For Eco, the cultural code itself is a network of contiguous surfaces objectively determined by the material density of cultural life. The items of the cultural code acquire significance by virtue of the arbitrary relations of their juxtaposition. The metaphoric structure of resemblances by which we order this code is necessarily an afterthought or a procedure of naturalization.

A metaphor can be invented because language in its process of unlimited semiosis, constitutes a multi-dimensional network of metonymies each of which is explained by a cultural convention rather than an original resemblance. The imagination would be incapable of inventing or recognizing a metaphor if culture, under the form of a possible structure of the Global Semantic System, did not provide it with the subjacent network of arbitrarily stipulated contiguities.[8]

Because metaphoric possibility is a product of contiguity, invention is confined not to a prior taxonomic base of resemblances but to constitutive features of contextual wholes: with the caveat that these wholes are strictly provisional. As Gilles Deleuze says of the metaphoric-metonymic basis of what he calls the *antilogos* style in Proust, "An associative incongruous chain is unified only by a creative viewpoint which itself takes the role of an incongruous part within the whole."[9] The whole is conceived to be not a causal contingency but rather a multirelational contingency of the concept of cause. The work is not an organic unity except as parts and whole are reconciled in the *process* of creation. I have sought to collapse *mythos* into *mimesis* (plot and creative act), and I have contested the dualistic habits of mind conditioned in narratological theory because I want to find a causal imperative more consistent with the rhetorical forms of the fiction I have discussed here. Because meaning in the case of these texts is multirelational, it is not easily confined to the taxonomic grids of a structuralist approach. As Eco and Deleuze suggest, the causal imperative on which orthodox metaphoric logic appears to be based (and I take metaphoric logic to be analogous to linear narrative) is inadequate insofar as it is invariably the disguise of more complex relations.

The best way to focus my methodological disagreement with Chatman et al. may be to observe how our attempts to theorize the organizational principles of narrative hinge on the use of the term contingency. Recall that my description of the figurative density in Barnes, Hawkes, and Beckett (as retextualizing the contingencies of specific discursive practices) depended on tracing figurative determinations through a network of subjacent contiguities. In the cases of Barnes, Hawkes, and Beckett, the retextualizing works through a syntactical overcoding of semantic values. Chatman, acutely aware of the need to specify an organizational principle adequate to nonrealistic decentered narrative forms as well as closed realistic narratives, adopts Jean Pouillon's definition of contingency as: "depending for its existence, occurrence, character, etc. on something not yet certain."[10] Since it stresses provisionality of structure, however, such a concept would seem to make sense as a formal analytic tool only if we conceived form to display the constitutive discursive forces of a text. The narratological analytical framework, by privileging event as a threshold of knowledge, appears to be incompatible with the epistemological thrust of the term contingency precisely because the order of the event is not submitted to rigorous scrutiny of its own contingencies. There is no way to examine constitutive powers of the text.

In such an analysis, then, I am seeking a way to examine the constitutive powers of a text because I want to make it possible to see the narrative event as a product of diverse discursive forces, not as a holistic unity. In my own argument, the term contingency figures as centrally as it does for Chatman. And my own use of the term accords with Chatman's (Pouillon's) definition. But within the framework of the nondualistic notion of form offered by the texts discussed here, contingency specifies a relational structure that is not resolvable according to predetermined schematic relations. The distinguishing trait of these narratives is discontinuity, or narrative gap—that is, a contingency without a *logos*. Narrative event is intelligible through contextual irruptions. Therefore, event in the gapped discourse is not a privileged level of analysis. On the contrary, the predisposition to see contingency as an organizational principle confers a methodological sanction to explore levels other than event by disclosing the multiple determinations of that category. And since self-conscious novelists take the presuppositions of event—chiefly the authorial event—as primary, we need a methodological course that can scrupulously direct us to the determinations of our determinations. On this basis, I have argued that our desire to pinpoint an organizational principle for narrative must be situated within an epistemological matrix more complex than the dualistic analysis that narratology affords.

The search for a new causal imperative to explain the organizational priorities of narrative ushers in such an epistemological framework. The difference between the two admittedly heuristic models of narrative form—orthodox and avant-garde —that I have played against each other in this book is the difference between a set of meaning relations that is assimilable to a prior order and one that is bound diversely by contradictory principles of operation. In the distinction between these two modes of narrative (and the two modes of metaphor by which I have explicated them), a further implied distinction appears between act conceived as the outgrowth of motive and act conceived as a locus of motivation. This is because any notion of the production of meaning entails an explanation of agency. *Mimesis* is imitation for Aristotle. But if we discredit the correspondence theory of imitation that grew out of the critical commonplace "art imitates life," and if, like Joyce and Ricoeur, we understand the word *mimesis* to denote the creation of a structure for cognitive reflection equivalent to the productive capacities of nature, then we must also seek criteria for understanding the mimetic artifact that go beyond a theory of reference. Of course, this is Ricoeur's polemical dictum, not Aristotle's, though it should be clear by now how nimble a grasp of the formal structures examined in these pages Ricoeur has given us. The notion of act becomes relevant as soon as we see that the threshold of Ricoeur's *mimesis* is the transformation of contextual priorities and so demands a lucid distribution of motives.

The idea that the meanings accorded by contextual metamorphosis must be construed within a notion of act clearly is not new, although it acquires fresh urgency within the context of the narrative disruptions we have examined here. Kenneth Burke's dramatistic model of interpretation resourcefully engages questions about how we can adequately describe what happens in a literary text. He stresses the need to account for the creative energies exhibited by the text as act rather than representation, production rather than re-production. Burke, like Ricoeur, wants to understand how change of meaning (*epiphora*) occurs within conventionalized contexts of understanding or utterance without recourse to a regressive tautological order of resemblance. He attempts therefore to correct the notion that ends result from means in a simple relation of instrumentality whereby the properties of an act are intelligible only as they fit criteria of use. That notion is belied by both the formal innovations of the avant-garde novelist and our most spontaneous experience of the world.

> Agencies being related to purposes somewhat as motion is related to action, a statement when confined to terms of means and end eliminates "act" as a special locus of motives by treating the act simply as a means to an end. In a dramatist perspective, where the connotations of "to act" strategically overlap upon the connotations of "to be," action is not merely a *means of doing* but a *way of being*. And a way of being is substantival, not instrumental.[11]

Because he wants to establish act as a locus of motives, Burke offers a useful perspective within which to observe the project of avant-garde authors who stress the provisionality of any construction of events (that is, creation) predicated on a uniquely determined *telos*. It would probably be more accurate to say that ends determine our understanding of means in linear narrative, but the same dualistic hierarchy constrains our interpretation of actions. Like Barnes, Hawkes, and Beckett, Burke apprehends the danger of acknowledging that narrative events are products of mediating structures without submitting those structures to the situational mediations of every particular use of language. And yet this stance does not simply seek a demystification of the myth of closure. Rather, it is an unusually scrupulous way of showing how the act of giving priority to events over authorial acts—hence sublimating narrative desires—forecloses significant expressive possibilities; these writers express the desire to explore those possibilities. Therefore, we have good reason to link the formal novelties these writers execute with a desire to bring the text closer to the condition of act. If we wish to see act as a locus of motives, we are bound to a methodology that taps the expressive possibilities of contradiction by disallowing a simple sufficiency of act to purpose. Correspondingly, we observe in the narratives of Barnes, Hawkes, and Beckett a systematic overdetermination of the mediating conventions of plot, character, and setting—conventions that make possible the sufficiency of act to purpose. On this basis, I have asserted the relevance of an interpretive method situated at a rhetorical threshold where character, plot, and setting approach intelligibility only as they reveal the organizational priorities of their structure to be the dissimulation of other structural imperatives. Rhetoric in this sense connotes specifically the mechanism by which meaning is determined at the level of contextual change—hence my concentration on gaps as a significant organizational level.

I should add that we need not go back to Renaissance theorists of catachresis to find precedent for the idea that a logical gap has long been a significant juncture for the creators of fictional worlds. In his attempts to theorize the nature of creation in the novel, Henry James specifically refers to an essential estranging disruption of perceptions that seems distinctly analogous to the germinal *discordia concours* of all metaphor. His "Prefaces" assert a structural principle based on the ungoverned proliferation of scenic particulars and thus giving precedence to character over plot. James's stylistic provision for an incomplete assimilation of motives to facts guarantees expression of the full potentialities of act. In his ideal narrative, "the intensity of suggestion that may reside in the stray figure, the unattached character, the image *en disponibilité*" would be privileged above the contextual facts by which narrative developments are plotted.[12] Plot, that "nefarious word," is to James's mind a preemption of knowledge because it substitutes recognition for intellection. Writing about Joseph Conrad's rigorous denial of an authenticating point of view in *Chance*, James generalizes about the unique productive agency provided to the art form insofar as it can "glory in a gap."[13] As Burke implies, the fertility of this gap, opened by the suspension of teleological necessity, is seen in the proliferation of new motivational grounds.

The proliferation of new motivational grounds is precisely the rhetorical work of the novelists I have discussed. We have seen that the novelty of the experimental novelist is self-consciously foregrounded by a rhetorical "impropriety" that disjoins the tautological propositions of conventional trope. If we acknowledge a reason to unite *mimesis* with *mythos*, we can further understand how catachresis or extended trope offers a means of collapsing motive into act through its introduction of a productive gap. Motive, commonly harbored within the hypostatic causality of plot, is therefore displaced by catachrestic rhetoric to reflect the exigencies of contextual transformation that catachresis produces rather than names.

In one sense, this is merely a reaffirmation that novelty involves throwing off habits of consciousness. And this is certainly a universal assumption about significant literature. But we escape the banality of such a claim by realizing that this "throwing off" becomes part of consciousness only when consciousness itself ceases to be preconception. In Barnes, Hawkes, and Beckett, therefore, the particular enabling stratagems of estrangement become important for their own sake as they disclose how our habits of gaining experience function. This is chiefly what distinguishes them from their predecessors.

Furthermore, this focus permits us to comprehend the estrangements of radical forms as a reflexive knowledge about their conditions of possibility. Thus, if the terms of my analysis are not tuned to the jargon of a more popular critical inquiry stressing elements of form or taxonomies of function, it is because I take the discursive substratum of what I call "predicative authority" to be more fruitful critical ground. With the

term predicative authority I have designated the relation between predicates and the objects to which they can be applied
as a basis for mapping the transformations of contextual logic
organizing a text. This has led me to postulate that the positionality of the subject in discourse is a crucial determinant of
the meaning of narrative structure. Because "positionality"
presupposes a principle of mobility within the signifying matrix
of an established discourse, I have further implied that it will
illuminate the novel's relation to changing ideology. If we follow
the lead of critics of ideology such as Louis Althusser in the understanding that "the category of the subject is always constitutive of all ideology insofar as all ideology has the function
of constituting concrete individuals as subjects,"[14] then we
must find more enlightening ways to identify the positions that
specific narrative conventions make available to subjective
consciousness.

Obviously this study does not fully relate the models of subjectivity offered by avant-garde narrative styles with ideological modes of production. This is material for another book.
Nonetheless, I believe that the groundwork has been established here in my choice of a critical method that situates familiar questions about narrative logic at the level of production.
The act of creation is here revealed to be instructive about the
very cultural paradigms (privileging event) that in the past
have led us to take the meaning of novels for granted as merely
a cultural byproduct.

I am not claiming that the modern avant-garde novels constitute the sole proprietor of these insights. I am only arguing
that in the recent experimental novel, narrative prose bears
the burden of the tasks outlined above more conscientiously
than does the canon of, say, realist fiction. Furthermore, just as
Kenneth Burke does not conceive his act-as-locus-of-motivation
independently of the rest of the pentad, I am not proposing that
the experimental writer's self-consciousness about the epistemological status of fiction forecloses conventional meaning relations. Rather, I have shown how in specific cases rhetoric is

raised to the status of act by its reflexive dramatization of the productivity of the text. My point is that this practice displays a distinct variation on the kinds of knowledge that the genre typically makes available to a reader.

Appropriately, Barnes, Hawkes, and Beckett write fictions that are articulated by jeopardizing the very meaning-relations that signify their authorial power. Engaged as these writers are, at least theoretically, in revealing the basis of fiction, they are of course vulnerable to the tautological trap of their own fictionality. But this is after all the dilemma of any metaphoric knowledge. Thus, in the work of writers for whom such awareness is paramount, we find their formal experiments strictly confined to the authorial agency that they operate rather than to the illusory object-language that the genre has conjured as its historical justification. These authors constrain themselves to inhabit the gestures of their own meaning as gesture. As a result, the experience of contingency they explore does not simply open a window on the world; it endows a means of restructuring reality, making that act *qua* act intelligible in all its epistemological complexity.

NOTES

The bibliography contains the full references for note citations.

Chapter 1. The Fictions of Metaphor

1. See in particular chapter 14 of Coleridge's *Biographia Literaria*. This intuition remains intact even in radical postidealist reformulations of the concept of literary text. Georg Lukács, after the example of Hegel, posits poetry as a virtually uncontingent positivity, commensurable with the organic wholeness of classical Greek culture. Prose by contrast posits divided consciousness, a threshold of political alienation, the modern history of class struggle. The opposition of poetry and prose, at least in Lukács's Marxist period, posits simultaneously political nostalgia and esthetic utopianism. See particularly "Art and Objective Truth," in *Writer and Critic*, trans. Arthur D. Kahn (New York: Grosset and Dunlap, 1970).
2. Lubbock, *Craft of Fiction*, 254.
3. Booth, *Rhetoric of Fiction*, 20.
4. Freedman, *Lyrical Novel*, vii.
5. Ibid., 17.
6. de Man, *Allegories of Reading*, 10.
7. Derrida, "Structure, Sign and Play," 247–65.
8. Derrida, *Of Grammatology*, 6–87.
9. Derrida, *Dissemination*, 140.
10. Culler, *Structuralist Poetics*, 189–230.
11. Federman, "Surfiction," in *Surfiction*, ed. Federman, 8.
12. Barthes, *Pleasure*, 32.
13. Barthes, *Writing Degree Zero*, 69.
14. Barthes, *S/Z*, 80.
15. Ronald Sukenick, "The New Tradition in Fiction," in *Surfiction*, 44.
16. David Lodge, *Modes of Modern Writing*, 245.
17. Federman, "Surfiction," 9–15.
18. Barth, "The Literature of Exhaustion," in *Surfiction*, 28.
19. Derrida, "Structure, Sign and Play," 245–47.
20. Ibid., 245.
21. Barth, "Literature of Exhaustion," 29.
22. Ibid., 24–25.
23. Borges, *Ficciones*, 53.

24. I am following the practice of many theorists of the rhetorical school (de Man, Kristeva, Derrida) by using *trope* as a verb in order to stress its constitutive function in discourse.

25. Heath, *Nouveau Roman*, 24–37.

26. Borges, *Ficciones*, 55.

27. Barth, "The Literature of Exhaustion," 25.

Chapter 2. The Metaphors of Fiction

1. White, *Metahistory*, 37.

2. Black, *Models and Metaphors*, 38–44.

3. Heath, *Nouveau Roman*, 40.

4. Joyce, *Portrait*, 171.

5. Aristotle, *Poetics*, 67–68.

6. Joyce, *Workshop*, 3–4.

7. For insight into Joyce's motivation in "Epiphanies" see Stanislaus Joyce, *My Brother's Keeper*, 124–25.

8. Caudwell, *Illusion and Reality*, 272.

9. Ibid., 272.

10. Aristotle, *Rhetoric*, 109.

11. Ibid., 76.

12. Mukařovský, "Standard Language and Poetic Language," 43–44.

13. Joyce, *Portrait*, 171.

14. Paul Ricoeur, *Rule of Metaphor*, 98.

15. Bersani, *A Future for Astyanax*, 109.

16. Ricoeur, "Metaphor and the Main Problem of Hermeneutics," 109.

17. Joyce, *Critical Writings*, 145.

18. Ricoeur, "Metaphor and the Main Problem of Hermeneutics," 109.

19. For a historical and theoretical exposition of the relevant valences of this term, see Said, *Beginnings*, 83–84.

20. Jacques Derrida, "White Mythology," 1–69.

21. Ibid., 70.

22. Charles Altieri makes the best case that Derrida's preoccupation with ontological arguments tends to minimize his relevance for literary criticism: "It may well be the case that we have no absolutely secure grounds for truth, but the more important question is whether we need these grounds for coherent discourse, even on the self-reflective levels within which philosophical analysis takes place. Without such forms of truth, we may not be able to produce single, systematic accounts of human behavior capable of resisting sceptical attacks. But on procedural grounds, and within a model of appropriate senses it is the sceptic who

must face up to the burden of showing his relevance" (Altieri, *Act and Quality*, 40).

23. White, *Metahistory*, 7.

Chapter 3. The Horse Who Knew Too Much: Metaphor and the Narrative of Discontinuity in Nightwood

1. Page references to Barnes's *Nightwood* will be incorporated into the text.

2. Frank, *Widening Gyre*, 30.

3. For a full discussion of the relation of "having" to "being" in the Lacanian account of the Oedipal complex, see Lemaire, *Jacques Lacan*.

4. Lemaire, 129.

5. See my discussion in chapter five of the relevance of Lacan's concept of the Real.

6. T. S. Eliot, "Ulysses, Order and Myth," in *Selected Prose of T. S. Eliot*, 175–78.

7. Bersani, *A Future for Astyanax*, 130.

8. Under the rubric of the substitution theorem, I am invoking those theories of metaphor from Aristotle to Richards and Black which predicate the expressiveness of this trope upon a "field of associated commonplaces" (Black, *Models and Metaphors*, 63.) The vehicle may be substituted for a "proper" term precisely because it is already implicated in the field of associated commonplaces that the tenor denotes. For an examination of the limits of this model, see Ricoeur, "Metaphor and the Main Problem of Hermeneutics," 96–110.

9. Derrida, "White Mythology," 57.

10. Within the destabilized trope, the complementarity of tenor and vehicle is undermined. The vehicle is no longer comfortably assimilable within the scope of the originally prefigured tenor. Thus, instead of nourishing the literal intentionality of the tenor, this vehicle declares its own purpose within the discourse. The vehicle usurps the contextual ground of the trope by proliferating itself, and so the univocality of the generating sign is lost in the multiplicity of its dissemination.

11. Derrida, "White Mythology," 59.

12. Aristotle, *Rhetoric*, 171.

13. Ricoeur, "Metaphorical Process," 153.

14. I am indebted for this information to my colleague Susan Stewart.

15. See, for example, Scoot, *Djuna Barnes*, and Kannenstine, *Art of Djuna Barnes*.

16. The Valéryean analogy to music is adopted as a thematic framework

for reading *Nightwood* in Jack A. Hirschman, "The Orchestrated Novel: A Study of Poetic Devices in the Novels of Djuna Barnes and Herman Broch and the Influences of the Works of James Joyce upon Them" (Ph.D. dissertation, Indiana University, 1962).

Chapter 4. The Parody of Fate: Second Skin *and the Death of the Novel*

1. Flaubert, *Letters*, 170–88.
2. Conrad, "Henry James," 715–16.
3. Lukács, *Theory of the Novel*, 56–70.
4. Barthes, *S/Z*, 88–89.
5. Page references to Hawkes's *Second Skin* are included in the text.
6. Lukács, *Theory of the Novel*, 70–84.
7. Ibid., 69.
8. See, for example, vol. ix, chaps. 17–20, where Tristram tries to equate the time taken to read a passage with the time it took to execute the action, in Laurence Sterne, *Tristram Shandy* (New York: Pocket Library, 1957).
9. Barthes, *Writing Degree Zero*, 30.
10. See Graham, *Merrill Studies in "Second Skin."*
11. Macherey, *Theory of Literary Production*, 49.
12. For a discussion of Lukács's understanding of characterological fate, see Jameson, *Marxism and Form*, 160–205.
13. For a full discussion of Lacan's theory of the subject, see Coward and Ellis, *Language and Materialism*, 93–121.
14. See, especially, Lacan, "The Subversion of the Subject and the Dialectic of Desire in the Freudian Unconscious," in *Écrits*, 292–325.
15. Lacan, "The Signification of the Phallus," in *Écrits*, 287.
16. Hawkes, "Notes," 287.
17. See my discussion of the Oedipal complex in chapter two.
18. De Waelhens, *Schizophrenia*, 77–90.
19. See Ver Eecke's introduction to De Waelhens for a very lucid summary of these points.
20. See the discussion of narrative authority linked to a ground of "authorial norms" in Booth, *Rhetoric of Fiction*, 158–59.
21. Barthes, *S/Z*, 98.
22. Barthes, *Writing Degree Zero*, 39–40.
23. James, *Art of the Novel*, 321.

Chapter 5. The Need of the Present: How It Is with the Subject in Beckett's Novel

1. Esslin, *Samuel Beckett*, 20.

2. Bair, *Beckett*, 527.

3. Beckett and Duthuit, "Three Dialogues," 68.

4. Ibid.

5. Beckett, *Proust*, 8.

6. Ricoeur, *Rule of Metaphor*, 9–35.

7. Ibid., 37.

8. Ibid., 38.

9. Ibid.

10. Ibid., 40.

11. Page references to Beckett's *How It Is* are incorporated in the text.

12. Driver, "Beckett on the Madeleine," 51.

13. This term has significance for Lacan's exposition of subjective consciousness as well: ". . . it [the shifter] designates the subject of the enunciation (*énonciation*), but it does not signify it." "Subversion of the Subject and Dialectic of Desire," in *Écrits*, 298.

14. David Hesla, *Shape of Chaos*, 6.

15. Genette, *Narrative Discourse*, 161–211.

16. Kristeva, *Desire in Language*, 132.

17. Lemaire, *Jacques Lacan*, 60.

18. Lacan, *Écrits*, 156.

19. Kristeva, *Desire in Language*, 133.

20. This is attributed by Coward and Ellis in their *Language and Materialism*.

21. Kristeva, *Desire in Language*, 135.

22. For elaboration, see Lacan's "Subversion of the Subject and the Dialectic of Desire" in *Écrits*, 292–324.

23. Jameson, "Imaginary and Symbolic in Lacan," 390.

24. Kenneth Burke, "Rhetoric Old and New," 75.

25. Burke, *A Grammar of Motives*, 66.

26. Ben-Zvi, "Samuel Beckett, Fritz Mauthner and the Limits of Language," 186.

27. Beckett, *Proust*, 156.

28. Louis Althusser and Etienne Calibar, *Reading Capital*, trans. Ben Brewster (London: Verso, 1979), 188.

29. Ibid.

30. Althusser, *Lenin and Philosophy*, 162.

31. Coward and Ellis, *Language and Materialism*, 78.

32. Attributed by Linda Ben-Zvi in "Samuel Beckett, Fritz Mauthner and the Limits of Language."

Chapter 6. Narrative as Event and Act

1. I am not forgetting that the revolutionary pose struck by Robbe-Grillet in *For a New Novel* demanded a renunciation of metaphor. He linked metaphor to the falsification of existential reality that the *nouveau roman* reacted against. I hope it is clear that I would reply, with the Derrida of "White Mythology," that language is inherently metaphorical, intrinsically denying the epistemological neutrality of a natural language. But Robbe-Grillet's fiction (see, for example, *La Maison de Rendezvous*) provides its own disclaimer of the uncontaminated *res extensa* proffered by his earliest manifestoes. I take this apparent contradiction not as evidence of the author's self-deception but as evidence of the evolving complexity of his esthetic. I believe that the discrepancy between Robbe-Grillet's discussion of metaphor in *For a New Novel* and his later fiction might be satisfactorily explained in terms of the distinction between denominative and catachrestic models of metaphor that I have elucidated in this book.

2. Some exemplary works in this regard are Propp's *Morphology of the Folktale*, Greimas's *Semantique Structurale*, and Victor Erlich's *Russian Formalism: History and Doctrine*.

3. Chatman, *Story and Discourse*, 20.

4. Ricoeur, *Rule of Metaphor*, 9–43.

5. Culler, *Pursuit of Signs*, 170.

6. Ricoeur, "Metaphor and the Main Problem of Hermeneutics," 108.

7. I am thinking specifically of Jameson's recent book, *The Political Unconscious*.

8. Eco, *Role of the Reader*, 78.

9. Deleuze, *Proust and Signs*, 170.

10. Chatman, *Story and Discourse*, 47.

11. Burke, *A Grammar of Motives*, 310.

12. James, "Preface to *The Portrait of a Lady*," in *Art of the Novel*, 34.

13. James, *Theory of Fiction*, 254.

14. Althusser, *Lenin and Philosophy*, 171.

SELECTED
BIBLIOGRAPHY

Althusser, Louis. *Lenin and Philosophy*. Translated by Ben Brewster. New York: Monthly Review Press, 1971.

Althusser, Louis, and Balibar, Etienne. *Reading Capital*. Translated by Ben Brewster. London: Verso Editions, 1979.

Altieri, Charles. *Act and Quality: A Theory of Literary Meaning and Humanistic Understanding*. Amherst: University of Massachusetts Press, 1981.

Aristotle. *Poetics*. Translated by W. Hamilton Fyfe. Cambridge: Harvard University Press, 1962.

———. *Rhetoric*. Translated by Rhys Roberts. New York: Random House, 1954.

Bair, Deidre. *Samuel Beckett*. New York: Harcourt Brace Jovanovich, 1978.

Barnes, Djuna. *Nightwood*. New York: New Directions, 1937.

Barthes, Roland. *The Pleasure of the Text*. Translated by Richard Howard. New York: Hill and Wang, 1975.

———. *S/Z: An Essay*. Translated by Richard Miller. New York: Hill and Wang, 1974.

———. *Writing Degree Zero*. Translated by Annette Lavers and Colin Smith. New York: Hill and Wang, 1977.

Beckett, Samuel. *How It Is*. New York: Grove Press, 1966.

———. *Proust*. New York: Grove Press, 1931.

Beckett, Samuel, and Duthuit, Georges. "Three Dialogues." *Transition* 49 (1949): 61–74.

Ben-Zvi, Linda. "Samuel Beckett, Fritz Mauthner and the Limits of Language." *PMLA* (Summer 1980): 180–201.

Bersani, Leo. *A Future for Astyanax: Character and Desire in Literature*. Boston: Little, Brown, 1976.

Black, Max. *Models and Metaphors*. Ithaca: Cornell University Press, 1962.

Booth, Wayne. *The Rhetoric of Fiction*. Chicago: University of Chicago Press, 1961.

Borges, Jorge Luis. *Ficciones*. Translated by Anthony Kerrigan. New York: Grove Press, 1962.

Burke, Kenneth. *A Grammar of Motives*. Berkeley: University of California Press, 1969.

———. "Rhetoric Old and New." In *New Rhetorics*, 61–76. New York: Scribners, 1957.

Caudwell, Christopher. *Illusion and Reality: The Study of the Sources of Poetry*. London: ELM, 1973.

Chatman, Seymour. *Story and Discourse*. Ithaca: Cornell University Press, 1980.

Coleridge, Samuel T. *Biographia Literaria*, edited by J. Shawcross. 2 vols. Oxford: Oxford University Press, 1907.

Conrad, Joseph. "Henry James." In *The Portable Conrad*, edited by Morton Fabel, pp. 84–85. New York: Viking Press, 1968.

Coward, Rosalind, and Ellis, John. *Language and Materialism: Developments in Semiology and the Theory of the Subject*. London: Routledge & Kegan Paul, 1977.

Culler, Jonathan. *The Pursuit of Signs*. Ithaca: Cornell University Press, 1981.

———. *Structuralist Poetics*. Ithaca: Cornell University Press, 1975.

Deleuze, Gilles. *Proust and Signs*. Translated by Richard Howard. New York: Braziller, 1972.

de Man, Paul. *Allegories of Reading*. New Haven: Yale University Press, 1979.

Derrida, Jacques. *Dissemination*. Translated by Barbara Johnson. Chicago: University of Chicago Press, 1981.

———. *Of Grammatology*. Translated by Gayatri Spivak. Baltimore: Johns Hopkins University Press, 1976.

———. "Structure, Sign and Play in the Discourse of the Human Sciences." In *The Structuralist Controversy*, edited by Richard Macksey and Eugenio Donato, 247–64. Baltimore: Johns Hopkins University Press, 1970.

———. "White Mythology: Metaphor in the Text of Philosophy." Translated by F. C. T. Moore. *New Literary History* 6 (1974): 5–74.

De Waelhens, Alphonse. *Schizophrenia: A Philosophical Reflection on Lacan's Structuralist Interpretation*. Translated by Wilfried Ver Eecke. Pittsburgh: Duquesne University Press, 1978.

Driver, Tom. "Beckett on the Madeleine." *Columbia Forum* (Summer 1961): 49–58.

Eco, Umberto. *The Role of the Reader*. Bloomington: Indiana University Press, 1979.

Erlich, Victor. *Russian Formalism: History and Doctrine*. The Hague: Mouton, 1955.

Esslin, Martin, ed. *Samuel Beckett: A Collection of Critical Essays*. New York: Prentice-Hall, 1965.

Federman, Raymond, ed. *Surfiction*. Chicago: Swallow Press, 1975.

Flaubert, Gustave. *Letters*. Translated by Francis Steegmuller. Cambridge: Harvard University Press, 1979.

Frank, Joseph. *The Widening Gyre*. Bloomington: Indiana University Press, 1968.

Freedman, Ralph. *The Lyrical Novel*. Princeton: Princeton University Press, 1963.

Genette, Gérard. *Narrative Discourse: An Essay in Method*. Translated by Jane Lewin. Ithaca: Cornell University Press, 1980.

Graham, John, ed. *The Merrill Studies in "Second Skin"*. Columbus, Ohio: Charles E. Merrill, 1975.

Greimas, A. J. *Semantique Structurale*. Paris: Larousse, 1966.

Hawkes, John. "Notes on Writing a Novel." *TriQuarterly* 30 (1977): 109–26.

———. *Second Skin*. New York: New Directions, 1964.

Heath, Stephen. *The Nouveau Roman: A Study In the Practice of Writing*. London: Elek, 1972.

Hesla, David. *The Shape of Chaos: An Interpretation of the Art of Samuel Beckett*. Minneapolis: University of Minnesota Press, 1971.

James, Henry. *The Art of the Novel*. Edited by R. P. Blackmur. New York: Scribners, 1962.

———. *Theory of Fiction*. Edited by James E. Miller, Jr. Lincoln: University of Nebraska Press, 1972.

Jameson, Frederic. "Imaginary and Symbolic in Lacan: Marxism, Psychoanalytic Criticism and the Problem of the Subject." *Yale French Studies* 55/56 (1978): 338–95.

———. *Marxism and Form*. Princeton: Princeton University Press, 1971.

———. *The Political Unconscious*. Ithaca: Cornell University Press, 1981.

Joyce, James. *The Critical Writings*. Edited by Richard Ellmann. New York: Viking Press, 1959.

———. *A Portrait of the Artist as a Young Man*. New York: Viking Press, 1966.

———. *The Workshop of Dedalus*. Edited by Robert Scholes and Richard Kain. Evanston: Northwestern University Press, 1965.

Joyce, Stanislaus. *My Brother's Keeper*. Edited by Richard Ellman. New York: Viking Press, 1958.

Kannenstine, Louis F. *The Art of Djuna Barnes*. New York: Gotham, 1977.

180 A METAPHORICS OF FICTION

Kermode, Frank, ed. *Selected Prose of T. S. Eliot*. New York: Harcourt Brace Jovanovich, 1975.

Kristeva, Julia. *Desire in Language*. Translated by Thomas Gora, Alice Jardin, and Leon Roudiez. New York: Columbia University Press, 1980.

Lacan, Jacques. *Écrits, A Selection*. Translated by Alan Sheridan. New York: W. W. Norton, 1977.

Lemaire, Anika. *Jacques Lacan*. Translated by David Macey. London: Routledge & Kegan Paul, 1977.

Lodge, David. *The Modes of Modern Writing: Metaphor, Metonymy, and the Typology of Modern Literature*. Ithaca: Cornell University Press, 1978.

Lubbock, Percy. *The Craft of Fiction*. New York: Viking Press, 1957.

Lukács, Georg. *The Theory of the Novel*. Translated by Anna Bostock. Cambridge: MIT Press, 1971.

Macherey, Pierre. *A Theory of Literary Production*. Translated by Geoffrey Wall. London: Routledge & Kegan Paul, 1978.

Mukařovský, Jan. "Standard Language and Poetic Language." Translated by Paul L. Garvin. In *A Prague School Reader on Aesthetics, Literary Structure and Style*, edited by Paul L. Garvin. Washington, D.C.: Georgetown University Press, 1964.

Propp, Vladimir. *Morphology of the Folktale*. Bloomington: Indiana Research Center in Anthropology, 1958.

Ricoeur, Paul. "Metaphor and the Main Problem of Hermeneutics." *New Literary History* 6 (1974): 95–110.

———. "The Metaphorical Process as Cognition, Imagination, and Feeling." *Critical Inquiry* 1 (1978): 143–59.

———. *The Rule of Metaphor: An Interdisciplinary Study of the Creation of Meaning in Language*. Translated by Robert Czerny with Kathleen McLaughlin and John Costello, S.J. Toronto: University of Toronto Press, 1977.

Robbe-Grillet, Alain. *For A New Novel*. Translated by Richard Howard. New York: Grove Press, 1965.

Said, Edward. *Beginnings: Intention and Method*. New York: Basic Books, 1979.

Scholes, Robert. "A Conversation on *The Blood Oranges* between John Hawkes and Robert Scholes." *Novel* 3 (Spring 1972): 84–103.

Scoot, James. *Djuna Barnes*. Boston: Twayne, 1976.

White, Hayden. *Metahistory: The Historical Imagination in Nineteenth-Century Europe*. Baltimore: Johns Hopkins University Press, 1973.

INDEX

Althusser, Louis, 169; on causality and structure, 151–52
Altieri, Charles, 172 n. 22
Anagnoresis, 118
Aristotle, 1, 5, 13–14, 26, 36, 49, 54, 61, 125, 165; on good metaphor, 28–29, 173 n. 8; on proportional metaphor, 30; on *mimesis*, 122–23, 160–61
Authorial presence, 4, 28, 30, 60, 82, 99

Balzac, Honoré de, 10
Barnes, Djuna, 38–39, 47–78 passim, 80, 83, 163, 166, 167, 168, 170
Barth, John, 9, 20–22, 23–24; "The Literature of Exhaustion," 14–16
Barthelme, Donald, 9
Barthes, Roland, 6, 44, 109, 112; *S/Z*, 10; *Writing Degree Zero*, 10–11; on the reality effect, 82; on the preterite, 89
Beardsley, Monroe, 29
Beckett, Samuel, 38–39, 115–56 passim, 162, 163, 166, 167, 168, 170; on concept of action, 118–19; on *Proust*, 119–21, 137, 150–52
Bersani, Leo, 34, 55
Black, Max, 23, 29, 49, 173 n. 8
Booth, Wayne, 2, 8
Borges, Jorge Luis, 9; "Pierre Menard," 17–22
Burke, Kenneth, 149–51; on agency and act, 165–69

Catachresis, 25, 41, 45, 58, 83, 109, 158, 162, 167, 168
Caudwell, Christopher, 28, 30
Character: as facility of plot, 26; desire of, 55–56; transcendence of character-centered narrative, 65–66; conventional structure of, 84. *See also* Lukács
Chatman, Seymour, 160–61, 163–64
Coleridge, Samuel T., 1, 171 n. 1
Conrad, Joseph, 81–83. *See also* James
Culler, Jonathan, 8, 161

Deconstruction, 6–8, 18–19, 22, 41
Deleuze, Gilles, 163
de Man, Paul, 3–5, 159
Dénouement, 21, 26, 38, 77–105; parody of, in Hawkes, 103; identity principle of, 157–58
Derrida, Jacques, 6–8, 12, 21, 34, 159; on *supplement*, 15; on catachresis, 41–44, 58
Destabilized trope, 40, 43, 49, 60, 173 n. 10. *See also* Catachresis
De Waelhens, Alphonse, 50, 103
Dickens, Charles, 37–38, 98
Dissemination, 41–43
Duthuit, Georges, 117

Eco, Umberto, 162–63
Eliot, George, 53
Eliot, T. S., 52–53
Erlich, Victor, 160
Esslin, Martin, 116–117

Fabula-sujet, 160–61
Federman, Raymond, 9, 12
Ficelle, 112
Flaubert, Gustave, 80–83
Fontanier, Pierre, 58
Frank, Joseph, 47–48, 74–75
Freedman, Ralph, 2
Freud, Sigmund, 55, 93, 121; in Lacan, 100–101

Genette, Gérard, 135

Hawkes, John, 9, 34, 38–39, 79–114 passim, 163, 166, 167, 168, 170
Heath, Stephen, 24
Hesla, David, 133–34
Husserlian phenomenology, 133–34

Ideology, 79–80, 154, 169

Jakobson, Roman, 42, 62
James, Henry: on first person, 112; on structure, 167–68; on Conrad, 168
Jameson, Fredric, 161–62, 174 n. 12, 176 n. 7; on materialism, 142–43
Joyce, James, 9, 53, 165; *A Portrait*, 26–33; on *mimesis*, 35–36

Kanenstine, Louis F., 74
Kristeva, Julia, 6, 159; on the symbolic/semiotic functions, 138–41; on subject in process, 141–42, 154

Lacan, Jacques, 6; on Oedipus complex, 49–51; on engendering the subject, 100–103; as influence on Kristeva, 139; on Symbolic, Real, and Imaginary, 141–44; on shifter, 175 n. 13

Leavis, F. R., 36
Lemaire, Anika, 50
Lodge, David, 12–13, 22
Lubbock, Percy, 2
Lukács, Georg, 82, 85, 98

Macherey, Pierre, 92–93
Materialism, 142–44, 159. *See also* Jameson
Mauthner, Fritz, 150–51
Metafiction, 9, 12–14, 24, 25, 33, 36, 170
Metaphor, 5–6, 14–15, 23–46 passim, 57; theories of, 29–30; substitution theorem, 31, 35, 48; live versus dead, 33; and the Oedipal stage, 50, 101–2; as related to *lexis* and *poesis*, 122–23; predicative and denominative contrasted, 131. *See also* Catachresis; Ricoeur
Middlemarch, 39
Mimesis, 5, 7, 13, 35–36, 39, 130, 160–61, 163, 165, 168. *See also* Ricoeur
Mukařovský, Jan, 31
Mythos, 1, 26, 119, 160–61, 163, 168

Nabokov, Vladimir, 9
Narratology, 135, 158–65
Nietzsche, Friedrich, 141

Postmodernism, 12, 13–14
Pouillon, Jean, 164
Predicative authority, 85, 168–69
Production, 4–6

Quintillian, 28

Richards, I. A., 29, 49, 173 n. 8; on dynamic of tenor and vehicle, 40
Ricoeur, Paul, 29, 33, 128, 131, 153,

173 n. 8; on *mimesis*, 35, 121–24, 160–61, 165–66; on second-order reference, 62–63
Robbe-Grillet, Alain, 158, 176 n. 1
Ryle, Gilbert, 121

Sartre, J. P., 8
Scoot, James, 74
Shifter, 131, 175 n. 13
Spatial form, 48, 51, 74
Sterne, Laurence, and *Tristram Shandy*, 37–38, 88–89, 158, 174 n. 8
Structuralism, 6
Subject, subjectivity, 45, 50, 130, 115–56 passim; in Lacanian analysis, 50, 100–103; as locus of

rationality, 120; positionality of, 109, 144 (*see also* Shifter); in process, 169 (*see also* Kristeva)
Sukenick, Ronald, 11
Supplement, 15, 19, 58
Surfiction, 9, 11

Telos, teleology, 26, 30, 38; and metaphor, 30, 54; and thematic closure, 34–35; and image, 61; frustrated in *How It Is*, 124–25; and subjectivity, 130

Van Velde, Bram, 118, 130, 131

Watt, Ian, 8
White, Hayden, 44–45